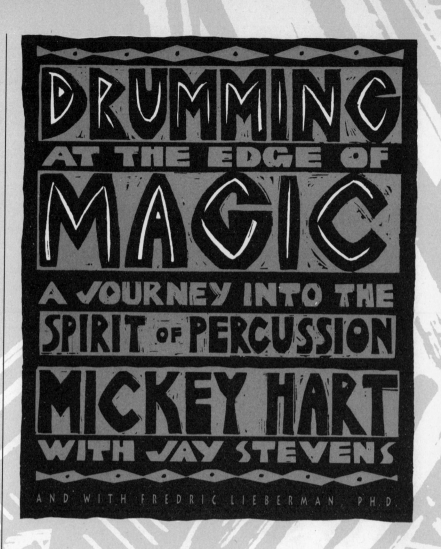

DRUMMING
AT THE EDGE OF
MAGIC
A JOURNEY INTO THE
SPIRIT OF PERCUSSION
MICKEY HART
WITH JAY STEVENS
AND WITH FREDRIC LIEBERMAN, PH.D.

 HarperSanFrancisco
A Division of HarperCollinsPublishers

TO

all those who feel the
power of the drum,
and don't know why.
To those who dance
to its rhythm.
To all the drummers
of the world,
known and unknown.
To all of them
and to you.

DRUMMING AT THE EDGE OF MAGIC
A Journey into the Spirit of Percussion
Copyright © 1990 by Mickey Hart. All rights reserved.
Printed in the United States of America. No part of this
book may be used or reproduced in any manner whatsoever
without written permission except in the case of brief
quotations embodied in critical articles and reviews.
For information address HarperCollins*Publishers,*
10 East 53rd Street, New York, NY 10022.

DESIGNED AND PRODUCED AT TRIAD
BY HOWARD JACOBSEN

FIRST EDITION

LIBRARY OF CONGRESS
CATALOGING-IN-PUBLICATION DATA
Hart, Mickey.
Drumming at the edge of magic : a journey into the
spirit of percussion / Mickey Hart with Jay Stevens and
with Fredric Lieberman. — 1st ed.
p. cm.
Includes bibliographical references.
ISBN 0-06-250372-3
ISBN 0-06-250374-X (pbk.)
1. Drum. 2. Folk music — History and criticism.
I. Stevens, Jay. II. Lieberman, Fredric. III. Title.
ML1035.H38 1990
786.9 — dc20
89 — 45985   CIP   MN

95 96 97 98 99 RRD(C) 10 9 8 7 6 5

CONTENTS

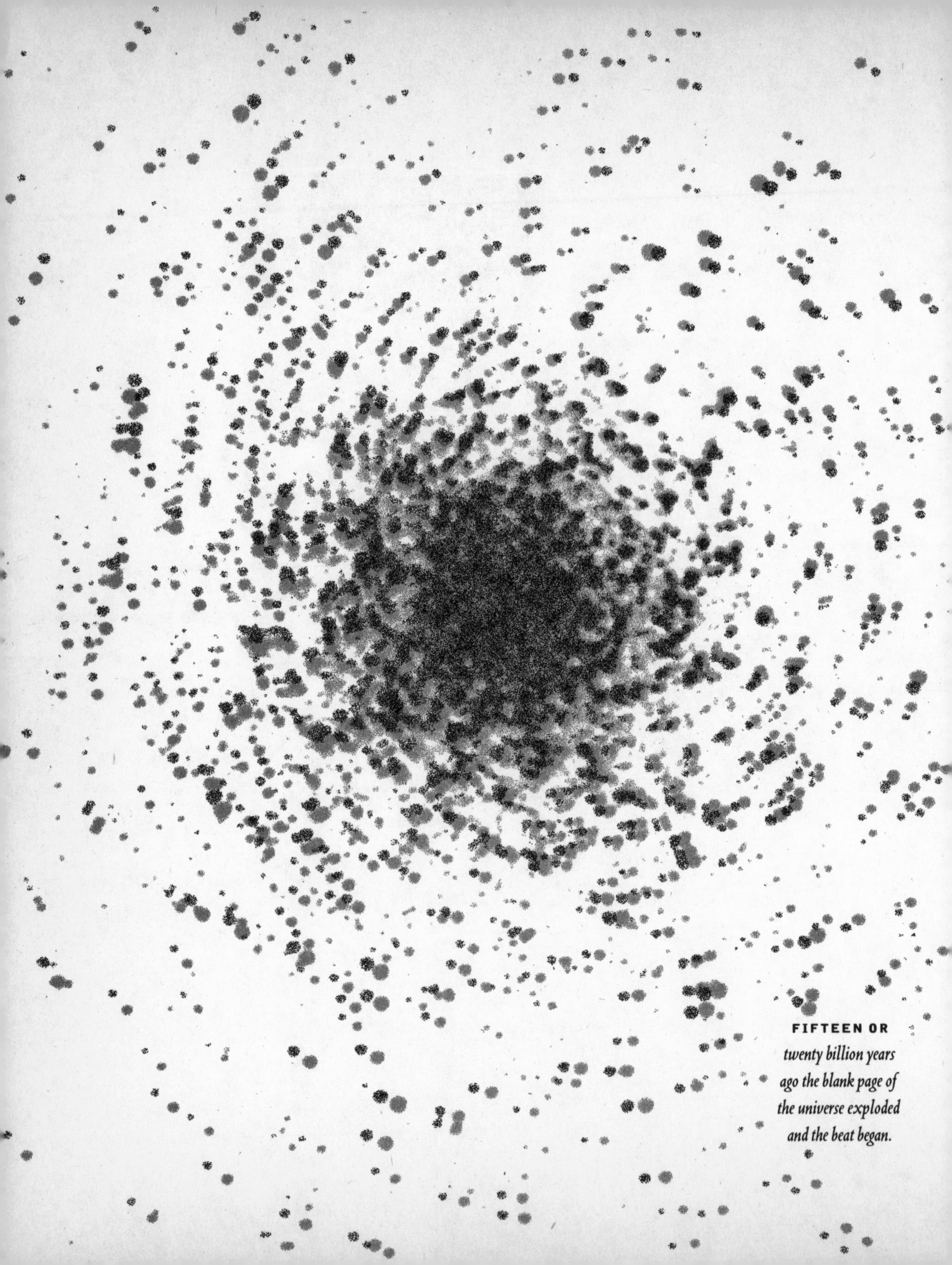

FIFTEEN OR
twenty billion years
ago the blank page of
the universe exploded
and the beat began.

Prologue

THE CONVENTIONAL wisdom maintains that fifteen or twenty billion years ago the blank page of the universe exploded and our story began. We call this fortunate event the big bang, which is a bit misleading as a name since the conditions for sound didn't arise until almost a billion years later, and the conditions for ears some time after that.

A better way of beginning might be to say that fifteen or twenty billion years ago the blank page of the universe exploded and the beat began, since what emerged from that thick soup of neutrinos and photons were rhythmic pulses vibrating through empty space, keying the formation of galaxies, solar systems, planets, us.

It is possible, however, that in the metaphorical and mathematical concept of the big bang we are unwittingly brushing against a larger truth. Hindus believe there is a seed sound at the heart of creation, the *Nada;* a passage in the *Tibetan Book of the Dead* describes the essence of reality as "reverberating like a thousand distant thunders."

In the beginning was noise. And noise begat rhythm. And rhythm begat everything else.

This is the kind of cosmology a drummer can live with.

Strike a membrane with a stick, the ear fills with noise – unmelodious, inharmonic sound. Strike it a second time, a third, you've got rhythm.

Fifty thousand years ago noise and rhythm came together and we began to talk. Our brains, after some million and a half years of hominid evolution, were fully formed, with two of the three capacities that would enable our rapid evolution already in place – the ability to store long-term memory and the ability to create symbols. We were toolmakers extraordinaire, with a significant repertoire of grunts, squeaks, barks, hums, rasps, growls – poised on the edge of a cultural explosion that would pitch us out of nature.

Everywhere we looked we saw rhythms, patterns moving through time – in the cycles of the stars and the migrations of animals, in the fruiting and withering of the plants we gathered and eventually domesticated. Rhythm was the heart of mystery. And probably nothing was more mysterious for the ancients than the fact that once a month, with the waxing of the moon, the women in the tribe began to bleed. And if they didn't bleed – that too was part of life's mysterious rhythm.

Imagine the soundscape fifty thousand years ago. Noise meant danger, possibly death, an understanding rooted in the oldest parts of the brain, in the fight-or-flight programs that activate the adrenals, preparing the organism for immediate action.

This is what the Hindus knew on a cosmic scale: there is terror in noise.

And in that terror there is also power. In one of her books, Jane Goodall tells of a chimpanzee who discovers the powerful effect of two empty kerosene cans banged together. Within weeks he becomes the troupe's dominant male.

Rhythm and noise. That's where drummers come from.

IN THE
*beginning was noise.
And noise begat
rhythm. And rhythm
begat everything else.
This is the kind of
cosmology a drummer
can live with.*

THE TAR
*is a frame drum
from the North
African desert.*

CHAPTER ONE

THE CALL OF THE DRUM

DAMARU IS A Tibetan ritual drum shaped like an hourglass. Technically it's a clapper drum, which means that it's not played with either the hand or a stick, but shaken. Two knotted cords whip back and forth against the two membranes, producing a sound somewhere between a buzz and a throb. The most distinctive *damarus* are made from human skulls.

In twenty years of drum collecting I've possessed only two *damarus*. The first was given to me by a friend who had purchased it in India, where a brisk market in Tibetan ritual objects has existed ever since the Dalai Lama led the Tibetan monks into exile there in the late fifties. This first

15

THE MOST
distinctive damarus
are made from
human skulls.

damaru nearly killed me – a story whose complete telling must await its proper place – and might have succeeded had not its rightful owner suddenly material-ized like something out of a Dr. Strange comic book, saying, "I hope you have been most careful, Mickey Hart. This is a drum of great, great power. It wakes the dead, you know."

I later acquired a second *damaru,* but was careful to get an unconse-crated, wooden one. I never played it. It gathered dust, pretty much forgotten, on the long shelf that held the smaller instruments in my drum collection.

FOR MANY YEARS I LIVED COMMUNALLY ON AN OLD RANCH ON thirty-two acres of government land in Novato, California, a town about thirty miles north of San Francisco. We were like an oasis on a caravan route; there were never fewer than a dozen faces at breakfast. When we first moved in, the property was scattered with ramshackle buildings in various stages of disrepair, the most impressive being a big cow barn with a concrete floor and wooden feed stanchions lining the walls – the Barn.

At one end of the Barn, we built a recording studio that was as close to state of the art as I could afford. The rest of the space, which was extravagant, I turned into a sanctuary where I could hang out with my friends and my drums. Some people like to have lots of cats and dogs around, or art on the walls, or shelves full of mementos. I like drums; they calm me.

In the center of the Barn was a fireplace/stove made from an old ocean buoy. With the lights off it looked like a glowing dragon's eye in the middle of an immense dark cave. Late at night that's where I could usually be found, sit-ting in my favorite chair, playing a drum.

I long ago abandoned my resolution to learn the voice of every drum in my collection. Life got too complicated for that. It's an amusement I'm sav-ing for my twilight years. Everybody else in the nursing home will be wired up to the communal stimulation unit, and I'll be in the corner, senile and tooth-less, playing my *tar*.

I never set out to become a drum collector; it just happened. I'd had gongs and congas around for years, but after my adventure with that first *damaru,* I began asking friends to keep an eye out for any interesting drums they might encounter in their travels. Eventually a regular buying network formed, composed of people like the gem dealer from San Francisco, who flew regularly into the South Sea islands to buy precious stones, and another friend in Italy, who was well placed to acquire the percussive instruments of Africa – the mother lode for us rock and roll drummers – and the drums began to arrive. I wasn't gathering these drums to look at them, though their shape and decoration were fascinating. I wanted to *play* them. I wanted to learn the secrets of their higher voices.

You might say drums have two voices. One is technical, having to do with the drum's shape, the material it's made of, its cultural context, and the standard way it's played. Technique gives you this voice – the drum's sweet spot, that point where the drummer, the drumhead, and the rhythm that arises from their interaction flow seamlessly together. It takes commitment and apprenticeship to learn how to find a drum's sweet spot. But once you do, the potential arises for contacting the drum's second voice – one I have come to think of as the spirit side of the drum.

Exploring the spirit side of the drum has been the major adventure of my adulthood, if not my whole life. From the age of ten until forty, all I did was drum. Obsessively. Passionately. Painfully. For a long time the drum took everything I had; it had all my attention. The call of the drum was the one constant in a life of such chaos that my head aches just remembering it.

I MAKE MY LIVING AS A PERFORMER OF POPULAR MUSIC, PRINCIPALLY as one of the two drummers in the Grateful Dead. I can't deny that I've lucked out in my choice of profession. The backbeat has been good to me. It's made it possible, so far at least, to fully live out the life of my imagination. For a long time that was all I lived for.

My imagination has always been fed by sound and by that higher craft of sound, music. I have always been synesthetic, which means I see sounds and hear images. A flight of birds, for instance, can become a rippling rhythm of notes, while a rhythmic pattern played on the Egyptian *tar* can become a flight of birds riding the desert thermals.

As soon as I could afford it, I acquired the equipment that would allow me to preserve these moments. If the drum was my public instrument, the studio at the Barn became my private one. Dan Healy, the Grateful Dead's sound engineer, and I built it so it was always on; all I had to do was punch one button and I was ready to record – like a fireman, into my coat and down the pole within seconds of the first alarm.

I was like an antenna, always scanning for musical information. I would disappear into the studio for hours, for days, burning deeper and deeper into those perceptual states where the magical can happen. I once spent weeks investigating the aural possibilities of insects collected from my garden. At night I dreamed music.

My bandmate Jerry Garcia once told me he saw me as "a mad Magyar dashing across the steppes." Apparently that's how I looked to even a sympathetic friend. My sense was that if I was in constant motion, building instruments, burning in the studio, playing drums all night, it was because I feared that if I stopped I would die.

I rarely read a book or went to the movies, and I socialized only when I couldn't avoid it. Self-absorbed, self-contained, I registered the ranch's usual craziness only when it conflicted with the single-minded pursuit of my own projects.

That's where I was at on the night this story formally began.

The Barn was one of those seductive spaces that naturally attracted a crowd. People were always asking to use it. There was always something going on – a recording session, a healing ceremony. About ten years ago, a planning committee that was organizing a benefit for the Vietnam veterans of the Bay Area held a pre-benefit working party there. Twenty or thirty strangers, many of them old sixties radicals, came together once again to brood over one of the most passionate issues of our youth, which made my job as host a sensitive one. What was needed, I decided, was a soothing, reflective soundtrack – the sound of the *tar*.

The *tar* is a frame drum from the North African desert. Before playing it, the membrane, usually goatskin, is gently heated over a fire until it contracts to the proper tension. Then you address it with the fingertips, delicately. I ruined more *tars* than I care to admit before I caught its soft sensual voice. But once I'd mastered it I seldom went anywhere without one.

One of the *tar's* unique qualities is its ability to evoke the aural landscape of its origin – the dry, whispering air, the sun melting into the patter of

THE BACKBEAT

has been good to me.

rain on the dunes. I was pittering here, pattering there, when I noticed a curly-haired man take my *damaru* from its obscure niche and give it a good shake.

Binnnnggg . . . Gunnnngggg . . . Gunnnngggg . . . Binnnnggg!

I dashed across the room and yanked it from his startled hands.

"This is not a plaything! I know it looks like a toy, but it's not, it's a power drum."

People crowded around before the mad Magyar could erupt again. A woman wearing an astonishing amount of jewelry reached out a glittery hand to touch the little drum.

"A power drum? That's fascinating. Where does it come from?"

I was about to answer when the curly-haired fellow said, "It's a *damaru* from Tibet, though not a particularly unusual one."

I had only an instant to register my astonishment – what did this civilian know about *damarus?* – before the woman, pointedly ignoring the civilian, asked,

"What's a *damaru*, Mickey?"

Ordinarily there was nothing I liked better than talking about drums. I thought of myself as an expert. Certainly I knew more about the planet's percussion than most of the drummers I had met, and my *damaru* rap was one of my best, full of tales of exotic Tibetan lamas performing the arcane rituals necessary to awaken the drum's higher powers.

But this time it didn't hold together. One or two thoughtful, pointed questions from the curly-haired civilian left me groping for words that just weren't there. I felt like the victim of a perfect judo throw. One minute I had been stepping confidently into the center of the ring, the next I was lying on the mat, watching the ceiling lights spin.

"Who is that guy?" I asked a friend I'd seen talking with him.

"He's a composer and a student of ethnomusicology at Stanford," she said.

"Ethno*what?*"

"Ethnomusicology, Mickey. An ethnomusicologist is someone who studies the role of music in traditional, non-Western cultures."

"So this guy might really know about *damarus?*"

"If anybody'd know about *damarus*, Mickey, it'd be an ethnomusicologist."

One incident among many that weekend. I soon forgot about it, or so I thought.

FOR ALMOST AS LONG AS I CAN REMEMBER, PLAYING THE DRUM HAS stimulated certain changes in my consciousness — my body awareness starts to fade, time disappears, instead of blood it feels like some other juice is pumping through my veins. But suddenly it wasn't happening. I was like a bird who wakes up one morning and finds his wings won't work. Every time I tried to flow into this familiar state I was jerked back to face an uncomfortable feeling:

Look at you. You've surrounded yourself with drums. But what do you really know about any of them?

To which my response was:

The real knowing is in the playing. Drums give up their true secrets only to players, not to Ph.D.s.

The South American *surdo,* for example, looks like an enormous soda can. It's a *carnaval* drum; you have seen it in movies about Rio de Janeiro. But only a player knows that a *surdo* excites something in the feet; playing it is like walking on hot coals. For some reason your feet just want to leap into the air.

Or take gongs. A good gong has extraordinary synesthetic powers. Strike one hard and it bellows like a big cat. Some of my gongs have tigers in them; it can scare the hell out of you the first time you merge with the sound and a tiger leaps out roaring. But they also have monks in them. My gongs transport me to a forest full of animals, watery pools, and hooded monks.

And then there's the South American *berimbau,* the single-stringed musical bow. The *berimbau* doesn't make a loud sound, but it's a remarkably penetrating one. You can hear it a long way off, like a snake hissing in the jungle. Most instruments that work on your inner core have to be loud. Not the *berimbau.*

These instruments are capable of releasing certain energies that you contact only when you play.

But what do you really know about those energies, except that they exist? Do you know who made these drums, or why? Or even where?

ONE OF THE BARN'S LUXURIES WAS WALL SPACE. I HAD CLIPPINGS and notes all over the place; most of the time it looked like a giant bulletin board. I cleared a space and pinned up some Polaroid pictures I'd taken of my drum collection. Then I wrote down everything I knew about each drum on a piece of paper and tacked it under the appropriate picture.

Most of what I knew, when I actually committed it to paper, turned out to be little better than rumor – fanciful folklore picked up from the people who had sold me the drums or from other drummers I met backstage during fifteen years worth of performing.

I had never been much of a reader. I'd kept up technically with what was going on in the field of audio recording, and I'd read or skimmed or at least listened to someone who had read or skimmed most of the spiritual quest books that began appearing in the sixties. Nevertheless, I began buying books. James Blades on the history of percussion. Curt Sachs on the origins of rhythm. John Chernoff on the African drum. Instead of sitting by the fire playing the *tar,* I sat in my favorite chair reading a book. It wasn't easy for me. I've experimented with lots of meditative techniques, but learning how to slow myself down to the state of alert stillness that reading requires was one of the most difficult disciplines I have ever attempted.

The next thing I knew, I was buying notebooks, the cheap student kind, and filling them with what I thought of as clues, although at this point I had no idea what the mystery was, just that something had shifted inside me, revealing a burning desire to know.

To know the origin of the drum. To know where it came from, how it was used. To know why, in particular, the tradition of drumming I inherited as a young American percussionist in the fifties had become devoid of the spirit or trance side of the drum, a side recognized by almost every culture on the planet. I knew I was a practitioner of an ancient art, perhaps the oldest form of music making on earth, an art form that stretched back – who knew how far back it went? – and yet it was an art form that in my tradition had been fragmented, forgotten, lost in our culture. Why hadn't the ecstatic use of the drum penetrated Western musical tradition?

I was doing so much reading so fast that my eyes ached all the time. My fingers ached too, from writer's cramp. It felt like I was falling into my head. One morning I woke up in a pool of blood. The book I'd been reading – Blades's *Percussion Instruments and Their History* – was soaked. Apparently I had

THE REAL *knowing is in the playing. Gong, surdo (lower left), berimbau (lower right).*

fallen asleep in mid-sentence and had come crashing down on my nose. Who knows how long I had lain there. The clock said 5 A.M.

I got a washcloth, wiped the blood off the table, then pressed it to my throbbing nose. It occurred to me that maybe I was going crazy. I wasn't a reader. I'd spent most of high school cutting classes, hiding out in the band room. So why was this happening?

Then I remembered the party for the Vietnam veterans, the curly-haired Ethno, the *damaru*.

Binnnngggg . . . Gunnnngggg!

This is a drum of great, great power, Mickey Hart. It wakes the dead, you know.

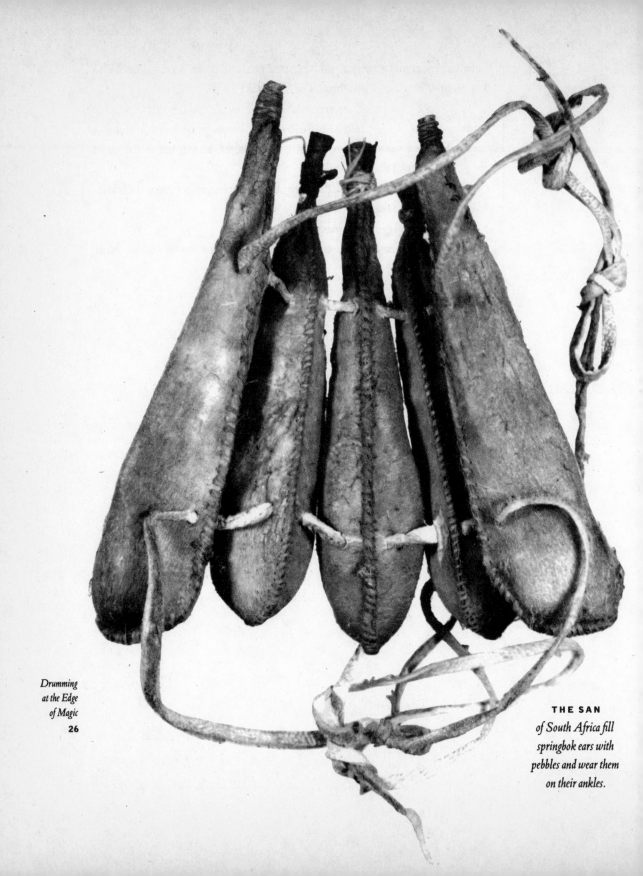

THE SAN
*of South Africa fill
springbok ears with
pebbles and wear them
on their ankles.*

CHAPTER TWO

THE GARDEN OF PERCUSSION

HE EAR IS THE BRAIN'S antenna, a part of the brain poking out into the world, always on, scanning for information in the form of vibrations. What we call sound is simply the limited spectrum of vibrations that this antenna can register.

As a drummer, I make my living producing a certain kind of vibration, a certain kind of sound. Although there are percussion instruments that can be tuned to specific pitches, most drums produce a sound that shotguns out in a wide range of pitches. This scatter causes the drumbeat's energy to decay much faster than do sounds that are vibrating close to a single frequency, leaving us with the kind of short, sharp sound bite that is perfect for laying down a rhythm.

27

The brain scans this scatter for information, searching for a pleasing pattern, finds none, and declares the sound noise. Drummers are noise makers, not tone makers. We are explorers of one of noise's most interesting qualities: the ability to create rhythms. And rhythms are of sufficient interest to us that information about them is routed to a whole other part of the brain than information about tone or melody or meaning. Rhythm is one of the things we are coded to scan for.

Words are so inadequate at capturing the spirit of percussion. Prose is okay at eyeplay; it can recreate the visual, but it's lousy at earplay. At one point in his history of percussion, James Blades digresses into a personal memory of "the attractive click click of the bamboo concussion sticks . . . in the hands of the Chow Chow man, plying his ways and wares through the streets of a busy Chinese city," and his book roars to life.

Attractive? Yes!

For want of the real thing, let that aural image fill your mind, the barking click click of the bamboo concussion sticks vibrating the cilia of your inner ear, sending electrical pulses streaming toward the cortex.

BLADES WAS MY BIBLE FOR A LONG TIME. HIS BOOK IS ENCYCLOPEDIC, five hundred pages of names, facts, dates — like a big tray of hors d'oeuvres, a nibble of this, a taste of that. I was so starved it all tasted good to me. But too often Blades would skim quickly over the stuff I was particularly interested in. He would mention, for example, that the frame drum was played by North American shamans when they sang their power songs, but then offer no further information about the relationship of drums to shamanic power. The other books I bought were just the same. The worldwide connection between percussion and ritual was alluded to everywhere, yet no one seemed particularly interested in following it up. "C'mon, guys," I felt like yelling. "Can't you see what's staring you in the face? Everywhere you look on the planet people are using drums to alter consciousness. How about a chapter on *that!*"

For a long time I thought I would walk into a bookstore and come out with a book explaining all of this. I finally sought guidance from several of my more learned friends who suggested I try a good research library. Have you ever been to a major research library, like Harvard's Widener or Berkeley's Doe? They're imposing stone structures, every inch of which hammers home the message that this is a very serious building. The first time I went into the library at Berkeley I felt as if I had entered a strange kind of church that was both very busy and very quiet – a kind of hushed, scurrying place. Everywhere you looked, serious people were praying over piles of books.

I couldn't wait to get my pile. I felt the same excitement that I remembered feeling when my grandfather took me to see the dinosaurs at the American Museum of Natural History – this was where the answers were kept.

My guide was a brisk, no-nonsense type with a Ph.D. Astonished that I'd never been inside a big library before, she was enough of a teacher to be moved by my sudden and naive eagerness for knowledge. Leading me over to a computer terminal, she punched in the topic – *percussion* – and scrolled quickly through the entries, jotting down numbers. I was captivated by the process, particularly by the fact that inside this immense medieval stone building pulsed a heart of high technology. In a minute we were trotting toward the stacks, zipping past aisles, checking numbers as we went.

We made a right turn down between two of the stacks and halted in front of a squared-off section of maybe two dozen books. The mother lode? I gazed at the titles. Blades was there, of course, along with Curt Sachs's *History of Musical Instruments* and John Chernoff's *African Rhythm and African Sensibility,* but there were also a few volumes I had never seen before. Eagerly I skimmed some of the tables of contents, my excitement fading as I went – there didn't seem to be much here.

Why were so many of the drum books so thin? And why, now that you mention it, were there so few? Why were there shelves full of books about the violin and walls full of books about the piano but only a dozen or so about drums, most of them monographs on obscurities like the gong in fourteenth-century Manchuria or gigantic tomes on narrow subjects like the *mbira* (the thumb piano) in Zaire.

I wheeled to question my guide, who nervously backed away murmuring something about there always being gaps in the scholarly record; if there weren't gaps, there'd be nothing for aspiring Ph.D.s to do.

A friend of mine, Remo Belli, who makes drumheads and drums, has concluded, after a long study of the global percussion market, that approximately one percent of the world's population are drummers. Which means, if Remo is correct, that there are probably a lot more drummers in the world than pianists, trombonists, or flautists. Add to this the fact that percussion is one of the oldest forms of music making that we know of, and you'd think you might have a ready-made market for books on the subject. But somewhere along the line something curious happened to percussion, as anyone who plays it knows. The drum got the reputation for attracting a more *elemental* personality type than, say, the flute or the guitar. I've heard the expression "Hey, whaddya expect, he's a drummer after all" in all kinds of places. It's generally said jokingly, but with an edge; even guitarists in heavy metal bands warn their daughters: "Just make sure you don't come home with a drummer."

It hadn't really bothered me that drummers were always relegated to the back of the band, but to suddenly learn that we were also in the back of the bus as far as music scholarship went — well, I was outraged, a little mad even.

Gaps.

I began raiding bookstores, particularly when the Grateful Dead was on tour, looking for anything even remotely connected with percussion — myths, legends, interesting lore, pictures. My equipment manager, Ram Rod, a wise and patient man who over the years has shepherded me through numerous enthusiasms, quickly adapted to the huge armloads of books I would hand him before the show — to be shipped home with the rest of my equipment.

Friends were put on notice. Anything having to do with drums encountered in the course of their miserable lives save for Mickey! I alerted my drum-buying network. Collect myths, lore, books, anything; bill me whatever it costs. I distributed a letter to Dead Heads through an electronic network:

Dear Friend:

I'm a drummer. I've been playing drums and other percussion instruments all my life. I've discovered, along with many others, the extraordinary power of music, particularly percussion, to influence the human mind and body. Many cultures have used percussion as a central part of their ritual and religious life. Much mythology and legend is concerned with the origins of percussion instruments, trying to explain the special power these instruments can exert.

You can help by collecting folktales, legends, myths, stories, proverbs, traditions about percussion instruments and their origins, uses, and powers. Send anything you find to me. Happy hunting, good luck, and many thanks,

Mickey Hart

And damned if it didn't work. The phone calls began, and my end of the conversation often sounded like this:

"That's great, let me find a pen . . . How do you spell Sumer? . . . A kettledrum mounted on an elephant? . . . Incredible."

Information lust. God, it was exciting. But after the first rush faded, a new anxiety appeared. What was I going to do with all this information? I imagined the way my predicament might read on a report card:

Although Michael has shown considerable improvement in his information-gathering skills, he still needs to work hard on his organizational abilities.

I FIRST MET FRANCIS FORD COPPOLA AT THE END OF THE SEVENTIES, when he hired the Grateful Dead's rhythm section, otherwise known as the Rhythm Devils, to work up a percussion score for the jungle sequences in *Apocalypse Now.* Later, knowing that I wanted to watch a film being made, Francis invited me to join him on the set of the movie – *The Outsiders* – that he was making in Oklahoma.

One afternoon, midway through my visit, Francis led me down a hall and into the room that was serving as his command post. The walls were covered with file cards. Coppola waved his arm in an encompassing gesture. "Here's the skeleton key to this movie. Every scene, every plot twist, every moment of crucial character development is right here on these cards. And the great thing about this technique is that you have enormous flexibility; you can experiment with different arrangements, you can . . ."

He suddenly became absorbed in what he had written on one of the cards. Not wanting to disturb him, I began to study the cards myself, slowly understanding that here was the solution to my problem. Coppola left a short time later, but I stayed in that room for hours.

The next morning I caught the first plane to San Francisco, leaving a brief good-bye note for Francis. On the way back to the ranch I pulled into a shopping center and bought thousands of index cards. Then I swung by a building supply store and left with nine or ten big sheets of pegboard roped to the roof of my car.

CRACK

*two sticks together—
or two bones—and
you've made a simple
idiophone.*

I leaned the pegboards against the old wooden feed stanchions in the Barn and began tacking up cards. I thought of this as my Timeline, although the principle of arrangement was much more complex than mere chronology. People would ask me what I was up to, and I'd hear myself saying things like, "Did you know that the sacrificial drums of the Ashanti of Ghana were covered with a membrane of human skin and decorated with human skulls?"

The Timeline grew like the beanstalk in the fairy tale. Within weeks it was sixty feet long. I even installed special lights, so I could work on any part I wanted. With the rest of the lights turned off, it looked like a glowing Anaconda that had coiled itself along the Barn's inner walls.

Where's Mickey? Out feeding his Timeline.

There is a moment in Steven Spielberg's *Close Encounters of the Third Kind* that always reminds me of myself during that period. It's the scene when the character played by Richard Dreyfuss, driven mad by this insistent image that has roared up in his mind, clears the family out of the house and builds what turns out to be Devil's Tower out of mud on the dining room table, while his horrified family watches from the windows.

In my case it was the Timeline.

All he does, Doctor, is sit out there all night long, reading those strange books and scribbling notes to himself that he then arranges and rearranges on the wall. This guy's a drummer, Doc. Drummers are simpler than the rest of us; they've got to be able to handle the backbeat. You've got to cure him before he drives us all crazy.

For once in my life I wanted interruption, craved it. Like the madman who holds the innocent wedding guest hostage, I would relate my tale to anyone who showed the slightest bit of interest in my Anaconda.

That's the way it was at the Barn: *You! Step into my garden of percussion.*

IF PERCUSSION IS THE ART OF STRIKING, THEN IDIOPHONES ARE THE oldest and the simplest tools in the percussionist's arsenal. Rattles, stampers, clappers, scrapers — these are all idiophones. Crack two sticks together — or two bones — and you've made a simple idiophone, which is any instrument that makes its sound from its own material, without a stretched skin or a string.

Dig a hole in the ground, place a board over it, stamp on it — you've made a stamping pit. Take two clamshells, clap them between your palms. Pick up the jawbone of a bison, rasp it with a femur. These are all idiophones.

In Papua New Guinea you'd hear the "clap clap" of shells and crayfish claws, while in Zaire the Vili would slap the thick expanse of their thighs with hollowed out baobabs.

Bwop . . . Bwop.

The San of South Africa fill springbok ears with pebbles and wear them on their ankles. In West Africa the top of a gourd is removed and the player pounds the open end against the ground, producing a nice percussive *pop!* as the trapped air vibrates against the fruit's tough skin.

The gourd can be kept intact and beaten with sticks or chopped in half, placed hollow down in the water, and struck. In northern Haiti players put metal thimbles on their fingers to excite the gourd's body, while in the Solomon Islands topless gourds are plunged in and out of water, making a sound that one writer transliterates as "uh-ah-uh-ah-uh-ah."

When I was a little boy my grandfather used to tell me stories of Africa that were full of drums, the famous "bush telegraph" of the old Tarzan movies.

"Dr. Boyce, I don't mean to alarm you, but it seems we were expected."

"How is that possible, Walters! Nobody knew we were coming. All we've seen for weeks are crocodiles and a few of these native chaps, and they couldn't have beaten us here."

"It seems the drums told them, sir."

"My God, the drums . . ."

The slit gongs, actually. Africa certainly has plenty of drums, but when the tribes wanted to send coded bursts of noise far across the jungle they used sophisticated wooden gongs capable of producing up to seven different tones.

A slit gong is basically a hollowed-out log with a slit, or several slits, carved into the top. Slit gongs can be as large as an elephant or as small as your forearm. Cultures that don't have skin drums satisfy their percussive longings with a rich variety of slit gongs. If you put your ear to a slit gong, you hear the same kind of faint roaring that you hear in a seashell. The voice of the gods, the voice of the dead, the voice of the unborn — each belief has its adherents.

Technically, a slit gong is an idiophone, as distinct from a membranophone (a skin drum), an aerophone (a trumpet), or a chordophone (a violin). These distinctions were elaborated in the thirties by the great musicologist Curt

IF YOU PUT
*your ear to a slit gong,
you hear the same kind
of faint roaring that
you hear in a seashell.
The voice of the gods,
the voice of the dead,
the voice of the unborn
— each belief has its
adherents.*

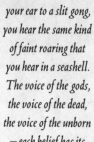

*The Garden
of Percussion*

STEP INTO
*my garden of
percussion.*

*The Garden
of Percussion*
37

Sachs, and they're a good example of scholars doing what they do best. But to a player, these distinctions are fairly meaningless. The Haitians play a clay pot in ways that encompass almost all of the musicological categories. Sometimes they beat on the pot with sticks – it's an idiophone. Sometimes they sing into it, thus distorting their voices – a sort of aerophone. And sometimes they cover the mouth with sheepskin or goatskin and it becomes a membranophone, which is the technical name for what most of us think of as a "drum."

Scholars believe that the earliest drum membranes were made from fish, snake, and lizard skin. Only much later did humans discover the tanned hides of animals. For me the discovery of the percussive possibilities of skin ranks right up there with the discovery of fire and the invention of the wheel.

The Australian aborigines, who technically don't have drums – they use mostly clapsticks and drone pipes – roll their leather cloaks into bundles and beat on them. The Xhosa of South Africa stretch a dried oxskin between poles that have been driven into the ground and drum on that. The Swazi take a pot and cover the mouth with goatskin; one man holds the skin while two others drum. The Hottentots have a similar device.

In East Africa coronation drums were only played with sticks made from human tibias. After the ceremony, the royal drummers would carry away all the drums except one. Whoever retrieved this seemingly forgotten drum was seized and killed, thus ensuring a never-ending supply of fresh tibias for future coronations.

In the South Pacific, I've read, the drum maker climbs the tree that is to furnish the wood for the drum and doesn't come down until the drum is finished. In Haiti it's believed that the wood for the drum must be collected at a precise phase of the moon, or else the drum will be vulnerable to termites. In parts of West Africa, the selected tree is fed an egg while the drum maker delivers this prayer: "I'm coming to cut you down and carve you up. Receive the egg and eat! Let me be able to cut and carve you! Do not let the iron cut me. Do not let me suffer in health."

A compulsion to drum has been loosed on this blue-green planet. The drums play in Japan when the rice is planted. They played in Cameroon when the king died and in the United States when an assassinated president was buried. In the Basque provinces the drum beats at the birth of the baby, and in Russia at the anniversary of the revolution.

Planet drum.

SCHOLARS
*classify the profusion
of drums by the shapes
of their bodies.*

Kettledrum

Cylinder drums

Goblet drums

Cone drum

AT NIGHT I STROLLED AROUND MY GARDEN, TAPPING THE *TAR* AND pruning the Timeline, transplanting bits of paper from one section to another. There was so much I didn't know, so many tantalizing fragments. When you're deep into the chase, certain creatures stand out like elusive butterflies. You can't help yourself. Whenever you spot one, you grab your net and go crashing through the underbrush.

That's the way it was with myths. I'd be reading along, brushing through the usual factual vegetation when suddenly, stepping over a fallen tree trunk, I'd come upon a myth in the middle of the trail:

HOW UNIVERSE MAKES RAIN

Double cone drum

One time when Big Raven was living on earth, it rained for so long that everything he owned got wet. His clothes and provisions began to rot. His underground house filled with water. At last he said to his eldest son, Emmemqut, "Universe must be doing something up there, let's fly up and see."

Hourglass drums

They went outside, put on their raven coats, and flew to Universe's place, where they heard the sound of a drum from within. It was Universe who was drumming. His wife, Rain Woman, was beside him. He had cut off her vulva and hung it on the drum. He had also cut off his penis and was using it as a drumstick. When he beat the drum, water poured from the vulva as rain.

Barrel drum

What the hell did that mean?

Usually I caught only glimpses – brilliant fragments – and when I tried to pursue them I discovered that the trail led back into some foreign language that I didn't read, like Russian or German or Serbo-Croatian.

Sometimes I struck a lode, though, and hauled in a real treasure. This is the way the Dan of West Africa describe the origin of their slit gong:

Frame drums

THE ORIGIN OF THE WOODEN DRUM

God created the wooden drum. It belongs to a large genie with one eye, one arm, and one leg, whose village is in a termite hill. This

genie chopped down trees and cleared the brush, and in the center of this open space he set the wooden drum.

One day an orphan left his village and went into the bush. Arriving at the genie's clearing he spotted the wooden drum. Two sticks were lying on it. The boy took the sticks and began to beat the wooden drum.

A genie stuck his head out of the termite mound and said, "Who told you to beat the wooden drum?"

"No one told me."

So the genie said, "Since you have already started to beat the drum, continue so that I may dance. If I dance and my feet get tired, you can kill me. But if my feet don't tire and your hands do, then I'll kill you."

The young boy beat on the wooden drum. The genie danced. When he got tired he went on the other side of the termite mound and a fresh genie popped out and resumed dancing. Eventually the boy tired, and the genie killed him.

Now this boy, though an orphan, had a younger brother. For three days the brother waited in the village for his older brother to return. When he didn't, the younger boy decided to go look for him. When he arrived in the genie's clearing, he saw the wooden drum and beside it the severed head of his brother. "What! Is this the head of my brother?" he said. "And what's this wooden thing on the ground with the two pretty sticks on it?" The younger brother picked up the sticks and began to beat on the drum.

Immediately a genie appeared and said, "Go ahead, beat on that drum while I dance. But if your hands get tired before my feet do, I will kill you."

The young man beat the drum; the genie danced and danced.

And he did something his brother didn't do. Whenever the genie danced around to the other side of the termite mound, the boy went with him. They circled for a long time. Finally the genie said, "My foot is tired. I'm going to dance with my shoulder."

The genie danced with his shoulder until that got tired. Then he danced with his neck. When that got tired he shook his arm. Then he said, "This is the day when it will happen."

"When what will happen?" asked the boy.

"I am tired all over, what more can I say?" said the genie.

Then the boy said, "The day has arrived for me to avenge the death of my older brother, whose head lies here in the dirt. I don't fear you."

And he killed the genie. Then he went around to the other side of the termite hill and set it on fire. All the genies died.

Picking up the wooden drum, the young man returned to his village.

Whenever I ransacked a bookstore now, I always stopped in the section devoted to mythology to see what was current. I noticed the name Joseph Campbell – how could I not? He owned half the section. One day I walked in and there was this enormous volume called *The Way of the Animal Powers*.

It overwhelmed me, as it should have. I had never read anything this powerful before. Here was a man writing at the top of his game, after fifty years of intense mental effort, offering his grand summation of our mythic substructures, probing into mysteries that go back tens of thousands of years where the only clues are some bones, some tools, and enigmatic paintings left on limestone caves.

Thirty pages into the book I was already thinking, "Wouldn't it be great to talk to this guy." By sixty pages I was calling around to see if anyone knew where Campbell lived. No one did.

At least once a week I'd be seized by the conviction that I should track Campbell down and ask him about drum myths. One day my phone rang. It was one of my friends, Betsy Cohen, shouting "Eureka!" They'd found Campbell and were inviting me to a dinner party that she and my bandmate Bob Weir were having for him. Would I like to come?

CHAPTER THREE

THE HOLE IN THE SKY

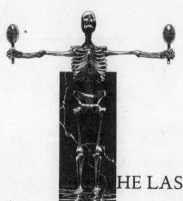

HE LAST TIME I SAW JOE Campbell, a few months before his death in 1987, he was as enthusiastic and entertaining as ever, inviting me to his house in Hawaii so we could finally sit down and crack open the mystery of shamans, the animal powers, and the drum.

Campbell never looked his age. He looked sixty-two, but he was over eighty. You could still see the athlete he'd been in his twenties in the way he carried himself, erect, balanced. Joe Campbell was the first intellectual I'd ever met who was also a warrior. For fifty years he had been burning away on the puzzle of myth, making himself, through his labors, one of the world's great

JOE CAMPBELL
*was the first
intellectual I'd ever met
who was also a
warrior. Left to
right: Campbell, Jerry
Garcia, Hart.*

comparative mythologists. Few people could see the pattern that connects – the similar and the synchronous – with his clarity and sweep.

Joe was convinced that we were about to remythologize ourselves. "A new mythos is coming," he used to say. "A global one, Mickey. I don't know how it will come or what it will be, but I do know it will not be unconnected to those mythic structures that preceded it, since the symbolic pattern of myth is at its root a reflection of the brain's own energy patterns."

Campbell saw himself as a mapmaker and storyteller, and the combination was impressive. He could have been an actor; he had all the tricks. But mostly he had a buoyant, vagrant intelligence. Limber him up with a meal of good steak followed by a scotch-and-water and he could dance all night, a ballet of the mind, leaping millennia, one minute back in the Aurignacian, the next right here talking about the Gaia hypothesis.

Campbell had added the mythic dimension to his sensitivities. He knew that the great myths were still resonating, however faintly, all about us, if only we would develop ears to hear this music. As far as Joe was concerned, we all had the potential to live out the hero's journey, if only we would take the first step and enter the dark wood of self-knowledge.

Adventures don't begin until you get into the forest. That first step is an act of faith. In his now-famous formulation, Joe used to put it this way: "Follow your bliss and doors will open where there were no doors before." Campbell lived his life according to this principle, and he urged everyone he met to try it. He was my kind of subversive.

AT THE PARTY AT WEIR'S HOUSE, CAMPBELL TURNED OUT TO BE THE graying giant, over six feet tall, who dominated the room with his exuberance. As Garcia later put it, "Campbell was a superstar; in any party he was the guy. He had a wonderful ego; he wasn't bothered if you'd read him or not. For myself, I was just delighted to meet the guy who'd written *A Skeleton Key to Finnegans Wake*."

And Joe was delighted to meet us. He had apparently tuned out of popular culture forty-five years before, devoting most of his time to his research. It was rumored that he hadn't seen a movie in years, and while he may have heard of a band called the Beatles, he was certainly unfamiliar with us. He could, however, give a stirring rendition of the myth from which our name is derived – the legend of the wayfarer who helps bury a corpse and then later comes into great fortune because of the service he provides to the grateful dead.

Campbell's first success as a writer came with a book written in the forties, *The Hero with a Thousand Faces*. It was his first attempt at mapping the mythic dimension, in this case the recurring story of the hero who goes on a journey and returns transformed. Thirty years after *The Hero* was published George Lucas was to find in it exactly what he needed to create a plot for the *Star Wars* trilogy. That a man who never went to the movies should provide the spark for three of the most successful films in movie history was an irony that Joe could appreciate, but he was still overwhelmed by it. Shortly before Weir's party, Lucas had sat him down and showed him the entire trilogy in one marathon sitting.

I worked my way up to him and at an opportune moment introduced myself, explaining that I was a drummer and one of my interests was drum myths. Campbell's eyes lit up. He knew all about drums and ritual. He knew that you didn't find a shaman without finding a drum. Years earlier he had edited Maya Deren's classic account of Haitian vôdun (or voodoo), *The Divine Horsemen*, remarking in his preface that nothing he had read had quite prepared him for Deren's personal account of possession trance, particularly "the power of the drums as they drove the god into the body of the devotee."

Joe knew about drums. He'd just never had time to run down the connection. It was a footnote in the back of his mind, one he had always wanted to pursue, and now here, at this improbable party, was just the guy to do it.

Joe explained all this later, twenty or thirty minutes after he'd launched, delighted by my question, into a story:

The Story of Morgon-Kara

Morgon-Kara was a Siberian shaman. He was so powerful that he could rescue souls from anywhere, even from heaven and hell. So nobody was getting to heaven because Morgon-Kara was curing everybody. Well, God didn't like that. "I'll get this guy," he said. So he took a woman's soul, put it in a bottle, and put his thumb over the top. Suddenly God heard a drumbeat, and up through the hole in the sky came Morgon-Kara. He saw that God had the soul in a bottle. Instantly he turned into a fly.

CAMPBELL
*knew that you didn't
find a shaman without
finding a drum.*

Have you ever been to the Arctic? There are flies up there that'll take a piece right out of you. And that's what Morgon-Kara did to God. He bit God on the forehead, and God said, "Oh, God!" and took his thumb off the bottle. Morgon-Kara scooped up the soul, hopped back onto his drum, and was riding back down to earth when God sent down a thunderbolt that cut his drum in half. And that's why the shaman's drum has only one head.

Was Joe one of my doors? Unquestionably. You encounter an elderly gentleman at a cocktail party, exchange letters, and meet perhaps a dozen more times before he dies, and it's as though a huge celestial body has passed too close to the earth, causing a permanent shift in everything, in the air you breathe, in the way you move through space.

AT JOE'S FUNERAL, A NEW YORK PUBLISHER INTRODUCED HIMSELF AND said, "So you're the guy who's on the drum quest."

That was just like Joe. One of the side effects of being around him was a tendency to begin seeing your life in mythic terms, a tendency Joe actively promoted. He liked teasing the mythic rhythms out of what you were experiencing as the usual chaos. From the very first, Joe made it clear that, in his mind at least, there was no doubt that the drum was taking me on a mythic quest; it had lured me into an unfamiliar forest — the forest of books and words and stories — and it was now my moral responsibility to accept this quest and dance the dance. Joe used to laugh, "At the very least you can write a book about it."

I loved it, but I also didn't take it too seriously.

"Joe, I'm just a drummer. I've never been to college."

"Don't talk to me about college. I taught college. College is wonderful. Everyone who wants to should get to go, whenever they want to. But you don't have to go to college to become an educated man, Mickey. You know when I did my best learning? Those five years I spent alone in that cabin in the Adirondacks, just reading the great works, Jung and Spengler, and the *Gita*. You know the *Gita*? I read through the Depression. I could have been doing other things, traveling, working. I could've started teaching. But the only thing I wanted to do was read. I'd fallen in love with myth, with the imago, you see. So in one sense it's the old story of the guy and girl. I was lucky, I had the time to pursue her. And so do you."

"But Joe, so much of the stuff isn't even in English."

"Hire a translator. That's what I do."

"I'd need people to show me where to look. I don't even know where to look for most of this stuff."

"These people exist. You can find them. Or maybe they'll find you."

Joe was an echo of the sixties that had aged so much it was wise and old by the time it arrived in the eighties to vibrate my memory, reminding me that things only get magical at the Edge.

I couldn't stop grinning as I drove home from Weir's that night. What a grand old guy. He reminded me of my grandfather.

EVEN THEN
*it was obvious that
the drum was the
most important
thing in my life.*

CHAPTER FOUR

Portrait Of A Rudimental Drummer

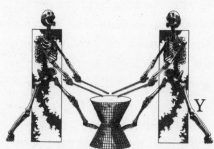

Y FATHER WAS A drummer, my mother too. They were rudimental drummers, which means they practiced a type of drumming that evolved out of a military tradition.

Every modern army developed a drum language – a kind of martial Morse code – to control the flow of the troops, whether they're marching between camps or in the thick of battle. The American military drummers developed twenty-six different rudiments, patterns of single and double strokes like the single paradiddle and the long roll. A good military drummer can manipulate the rudiments for hours, creating a soundscape that is simple enough to keep the troops in step yet sufficiently varied so they don't drift off.

51

Rudimental drumming became a sport in the early decades of this century, paralleling the rise of drum corps and the popularity of marching bands. The competition is comparable to a gymnastics event. Contestants are judged by two criteria: how well they execute the twenty-six basic rudiments and how creatively they can combine them into a medley.

My father, Lenny Hart, was a national and world champion rudimental drummer. My mother, Leah, took up drumming to get close to him; he was her drum teacher at the Coney Island American Legion drum and bugle corps, and together they won the mixed doubles competition at the 1939 World's Fair in New York. Two years later they married and settled in Brooklyn. I was born two years after that, but by then the marriage was over, and my father had vanished, leaving a hole in our lives.

We lived during those early years with my grandparents in Brooklyn. My mother worked as a bookkeeper, while my grandfather, Sam Tessel, drove a taxi. Grandfather wasn't an educated man — he had left school in the sixth grade to work, so reading and writing were difficult for him — but he read the *New York Times* every evening, and when I was little he told me fantastic stories, all of which took place in an Africa that existed solely in his imagination.

"We're across the Zambesi, Michael. Can you hear the drums? They've been beating since morning. Oh God! Why don't they stop? They're driving me crazy. And then, suddenly, they stop."

After the war my mother's brother, Uncle Sonny, moved back in with us. Uncle Sonny was a bugler, and one of the first things he did was rejoin his old drum and bugle corps. The five years after the end of World War II were the golden years of the American drum corps. The corps offered the mostly unemployed and bored GIs an innocent diversion that was still martial. A few months before they had been ducking bullets in the jungles of the South Pacific; now they were marching around green fields, beating the hell out of a drum, wailing on the bugle, hampers of beer and fried chicken in the car. It was fiercely competitive, incredibly noisy, and mostly male.

My grandfather loved the corps. It was more than a hobby for him. He was the unofficial dad of the Coney Island chapter. He made coffee, provided rides, chaperoned, counseled, and in return the boys named one of their tunes after him — "Tessel's Thunderer."

I loved the drum corps competitions. I used to run next to the bass drummers, bending low so the pulses of air would boom against my eardrums. It was at times like this that my father's name would inevitably come up, as everyone reminisced about the big, funny man who had been such a stylish and powerful drummer.

"What an incredible drummer Lenny was. Remember that long roll of his at 110 beats?"

It was as if they were talking about some drum god. My mother would grow quiet and sad, and the conversation would shift to a more pleasant topic.

I was ten years old the first time I ever saw my father. I was sitting in a movie theater, watching the Movietone News before the main feature, when a clip came on about the 1939 World's Fair, and for an instant I saw a tall, blonde man playing a drum. *World Champion Rudimental Drummer Leonard Hart.*

Whether anyone talked about him or not, I was acutely aware that I was the son of a great drummer. That was my father's legacy to me, that and his drum pad and a pair of beautiful snakewood sticks he'd won in competition.

The pad was an unremarkable forty-five-degree-angle wooden one, with a worn spot the size of a silver dollar in its center, the result of thousands of hours of precise concentration. I used to stare at this spot, with its moiré pattern of spider cracks, and daydream about the competitions that my mythical father had won. When I found the sticks, I began playing.

My mother used to hide the pad — at first, I thought, because it reminded her of Lenny. I was always having to search under the beds and through the closets until I found it again. My secret practice spot was in the closet, which acted as a resonator, amplifying the hollow thud of the pad.

Where's Mickey? In the closet with that pad.

My mother later told me that she hid the pad to test my determination. When it became clear I was serious, she agreed to teach me the family instrument, writing out the beginning rudiments on big index cards — the Long Roll, the Five-Stroke Roll, the Flam. Although she was careful not to discourage my passion, she couldn't hide her ambivalence about having another drummer in the house. In time, however, she became my greatest booster.

When I was ten or eleven I got my first real drum, a kind of classy toy drum that wasn't quite a professional instrument but it still gave me that first rush of drum noise. You either fall in love with the roar of the drum or you don't and drift off to something like the piccolo.

WHEN I WAS A FRESHMAN IN HIGH SCHOOL MY MOTHER AND I MOVED from Brooklyn to Lawrence, Long Island, and my apprenticeship to the drum began in earnest.

The first time I walked into the Lawrence band room sunlight was pouring through some high windows directly onto an enormous collection of big blue drums with gold-painted heads, blue and gold being the colors of the Lawrence "Golden Tornadoes." It was an incredible sight, like walking into King Tut's tomb if Tut had been a drummer. Field drums. Bass drums. But also tubas, sousaphones. And the smell. All those rotting mouthpieces. When no one else was in the band room I used to wander from drum to drum, inhaling that incredible perfume of paint and pounded leather. I think I decided then and there that this was what I wanted my life to smell like.

There was magic in that room, because there was a magician.

I'm convinced that Arthur Jones could have been anything he wanted to be. He could have been president. He even looked like a politician — he had that silver fox look — yet Jonesy had decided to spend this incarnation teaching band at Lawrence High School. He was one of the acknowledged princes of the school, a position he could have held solely on strength of personality. But it also didn't hurt that for four years he had produced the number one school band in the state of New York.

Band was a class like any other; people were in and out of the band room all day long, but if you wanted to find me, no matter what period it was, you looked in the band room first. This was not easy to achieve. I had people running all over the school dropping off passes that I forged from a thick stack of blank ones sold to me by a friend who ran them off on his printing press.

I fooled no one, I'm sure. Every month or so, the long arm of the principal would reach out and grab me, and I'd have to sit through another depressing lecture about what my life was going to be like as a deviant, until Jonesy arrived to bail me out.

"Oh come on, Kris. He's not going to be an English major. He's not going to be a lawyer. He's going to be a drummer. All he wants to do is drum. Give him a break."

Jonesy almost didn't let me in the band. When I applied he asked what instrument I wanted to play. I said I was a drummer. He groaned.

"Not another drummer, man. I've got twenty drummers already."

Jonesy always talked like a beatnik, though he wasn't one; it was just a role he liked to play with us kids. Everything was "like, man" or "hey, man,"

WHERE'S *Mickey? In the closet with that pad.*

though his verbal trademark was the creative contraction, words like "dasn't" and "unlessn't."

"I dasn't see how I can use another drummer."

I probably had terminal tragedy written all over my face because Jonesy instantly relented and asked me to play something. I walked over to one of the snare drums and played all the rudiments I knew. Years later Jonesy told me it was my intensity that persuaded him. Even then it was obvious that the drum was the most important thing in my life.

"I do need one more person in percussion," he said, "but it's like a special kind of job, man. Takes a special kind of cat."

Which is how I got the job of pulling the big bass drum in the marching band. Not playing it, but pulling it, like a mule – the drum on wheels, me in a white harness. I loved it. You've heard the kind of noise a marching band generates – the brass going *BBBBWWWWAAAAHHHH* and the drums *BOOM BOOM BOOM BOOM*. It's hard enough when you're learning an instrument to stay in time sitting in a chair; imagine learning to play and march at the same time.

That may be one reason why Jonesy approached life as a funny adventure. A sense of humor was much more important to him than perfection, though he believed that occasionally you could have both. Even when he was mad or wanted to teach you a lesson, he did it with humor.

We once had a big ceremony to celebrate our move into a new high school building. A priest had been brought in to deliver the benediction. I was behind and above the priest, on a riser, overlooking the rest of the orchestra, spacing out over some new timpani. I'd been waiting three years for these timps. They'd just arrived, they were right out of the box, and I was dying to hit them. As the man of God droned on, I could feel a powerful itch building, growing in intensity, until suddenly, out of the corner of my eye, I hallucinated Jonesy giving me the signal to roll. Up jumped my sticks, then down, like thundering horses, a sonic stampede. I could have screamed I was so energized by the noise. Then it registered. Everyone was staring at me. Particularly the priest, whom I'd cut off in mid-blessing.

I looked at Jonesy. He cocked his head and made a jerking motion above it with one hand, miming a hangman's noose. For three days he wouldn't let me in the band room. On every door he posted signs:

MICKEY! DON'T EVEN THINK OF COMING THROUGH THIS DOOR!

Or just:
MICKEY, DON'T!
Or:
DON'T EVEN!

MY MOTHER AND I LIVED IN THE ATTIC OF A BIG CAPE COD HOUSE that was owned by an Italian truck driver with five kids. I tried to limit my practice to when the truck driver was out, but I kept forgetting. My mother would hear him thundering up the stairs and bar the doorway with a broom, like a lioness protecting her cub. There was a cemetery behind the house that I cut through on my way to and from school. Since I always carried drumsticks I got into the habit of playing the gravestones. This earned me a neighborhood reputation as a strange and unsettling boy.

The years at Lawrence were a painful period for me socially. We were poor, and the girls I was attracted to were not; I couldn't imagine bringing any of them back to our attic apartment. Only the drum gave me the feeling of power and uniqueness that is so important to teenagers. When I had my drum I was the prince of noise, the loudest thing in the room, the loudest thing anywhere.

Jonesy let me try all the instruments – flute, trumpet, violin, trombone. My mother used to kid me, "How long will this one last?" Most were as fleeting as the typical teenage love affair. Two weeks and I'd be bored. I probably stayed the longest with the baritone horn, maybe six months or more. But in the end I always came back to the drum. It owned my imagination. I never closed my eyes and fantasized about becoming a great violinist or a great trumpet player. It was always a drummer.

Jonesy's empire – and music education in general – was rigidly structured. Newcomers started at the bottom. The bass drum was the first rung up the percussive ladder, followed by cymbals, tenor drums, and then the snare line, ten in number, which culminated in the first-chair drummer, who was considered the top drummer in the band. Every week Jonesy would give out assignments, and on Friday there would be an open competition to determine ranking. People moved up, people slid down. The Friday competitions were

electric. We were state champions, after all, and the mini-competitions we waged among ourselves were ultimately focused on honing our talents as a group, to keep the winning dynasty alive at Lawrence.

My hero, the best drummer in the school and the number one drummer in the state of New York starting in his sophomore year, was Brian Burke. A year ahead of me, Brian was everything I wasn't. He was a tall, suave, self-assured guy who drove around town in a chopped '39 Ford coupe filled with beautiful girls he would invite to his next gig. The most impressive thing about Brian, for me at least, was the fact that he had his own successful jazz combo.

Brian had a private teacher, Charles Perry, who had played with Tommy Dorsey. Perry had been wounded in the Korean War, so he no longer had the stamina to drive a big league dance band. Instead he turned to teaching and influenced a generation of young drummers who were growing up in New York and on Long Island. He was a tall, gray-haired man, with very smooth manners both with drumsticks and without. I begged my mother to let me take lessons from him, and although it was expensive and an inconvenience, twice a week Leah drove me over to Mr. Perry's house.

I was not a natural drummer; that's the way I remember it. It often seemed I was the slowest learner and the least talented member of the Lawrence percussion section. Nothing came easy to me; I was always practicing. After band practice I'd lug my drum over to where the cheerleaders were jumping and yelling and help them with their timing. Watching those angels dance to the rhythm of my drum was one of the most erotic moments of my teenage years. Then it was off home to beat along on my drums to Gene Krupa or the new Elvis Presley record.

My first drum set was affordable because the previous owner had bashed his foot through the bass drum. It cost thirty-five dollars. Besides the punctured bass drum, the set had a snare, a tiny Gene Krupa cymbal, a couple of hi-hat cymbals, and an old drummer's throne. Playing it was a revelation. It was like learning to dance sitting down, and it stimulated a new set of feelings. Mainly it wasn't martial; instead of marching all the time, you could swing, skip, shuffle, even rock. In fact, the drum set was invented precisely to accommodate these new rhythmic requirements.

Nearly a century ago, in the parishes around New Orleans, people began dancing to the new beat of jazz and the blues. Military drumming, rudimental drumming, was too rigid to power these new rhythms. In their search for an answer to this problem, drummers began ransacking the percussive

*Portrait of a
Rudimental
Drummer*

WITHIN
*twenty years virtuosos
on the "traps" began to
emerge, people like
New Orleans jazz
great Zutty Singleton
(at left).*

inventory. They took elements from all over the planet – snares and bass drums from Europe, the tom-tom from China, cymbals from Turkey – and along with such homely additions as cowbells, anvils, and woodblocks invented a new kind of drumming and, almost incidentally, a new instrument.

This hybrid was known as a "contraption," later shortened to "traps." Within twenty years virtuosos of the "traps" emerged, people like New Orleans jazz great Warren "Baby" Dodds, who worked with a bass drum, a snare, four cowbells, a cymbal, a tom-tom, and a woodblock. By the time the jazz age caught hold in the twenties, drum makers like the Ludwigs were already marketing formalized versions of the contraptions that drummers like Dodds had put together.

When I was learning to play my first drum set in the fifties, Gene Krupa and Buddy Rich were my particular heroes. Krupa, who was one of my mom's favorites, had played with the Big Bands of the twenties and thirties and, while not exactly pioneering the drum solo, he had certainly made it a climactic moment of every set. He liked working the low end of the register, the tom-toms in particular. He played, as the 1973 *New York Times* obituary put it, "with an almost fiendish zest as he flailed away at his snare drum, tom-toms and cymbals. Suddenly he would rear back, holding both arms in the air as he pounded his bass drum and foot pedal. And then, perspiration dripping from him like a tropical rainfall, his arms and drumsticks became a blur of motion as he built his solo to a crashing climax."

According to my mother, people would nearly pass out on the dance floor trying to ride these powerful rhythms. I used to put the famous 1939 Carnegie Hall performance of "Sing, Sing, Sing" on the phonograph and pound along with it, imagining myself driving the biggest, loudest, tastiest dance band that planet earth had ever heard.

Buddy Rich started out as a child prodigy in his parents' vaudeville act. He was three years old when his parents, "The Dancing Riches," wrote him into the act as "Traps, the Drum Wonder." Within ten years he was one of the highest paid drummers in the world, commanding fifteen hundred dollars a week, a serious little kid in a sailor suit who, whenever he got behind a drum set, erupted into a volcano of noise. In the early years Rich was almost invisible behind the big drums. All the audience saw was a little hand reaching up every now and then to swat the cymbal or tom-tom.

Buddy Rich extended what Krupa had pioneered, the complex interweaving of the percussive possibilities inherent in a drum set. The ride cymbal, the tom-toms, the snare, the hi-hat – Rich used them all, and he was fast and accurate. He played the bass drum like heavy artillery. And he never smiled. "Did you come to see my teeth or to hear me play?" he'd ask. He also boasted that he'd never taken a drum lesson in his life, and he rarely practiced. "All these guys get from practicing is tired wrists," he told one writer. "If you have something to play, you hear it in your heart and mind, and then you go and try it out in front of an audience."

I practiced constantly, rarely playing in public aside from school band concerts. My most intense moments with the drum were private ones. I would sit with my drums and slowly begin warming the traps up, exciting the low end first, the bass drum, making it beat like a heart, slow and steady. The hi-hat would start clicking its metronomic click, and I'd start mixing in the middle voice, the rhythms of the snare drums and the tom-toms interweaving with the steady pulse of the bass. This interweaving of low end and middle is the main work of a traps drummer; at the high end, the shimmering harmonics of cymbals, bells, and gongs complete the drum voice.

Ten minutes. Fifteen minutes. Twenty minutes. Then something curious would happen. I'd feel myself becoming lighter; I'd lose track of time. I realize now I was becoming entranced, but at the age of fifteen I had no idea what was going on. In my mind I connected it with an unusual experience that began when I was about five and that I associated, in my adolescent mind, with my grandfather's stories. For years, just before sleep, bright undulating bubbles would slip under the door of my room and float toward me. They weren't menacing bubbles, although sometimes they bumped against me, covering my face. Their appearance was accompanied by a tingling sensation in the top of my nose. And each bubble had a specific sound, a kind of high-pitched hum.

Eventually I learned the secret of controlling these bubbles. I could make them advance and retreat, and sometimes I could even project myself up into them and gaze down on my body. Now I was getting the same feeling from my drumming. I never found it exhausting to drum for hours; it left me calm, energized, and grinning.

My secret fantasy, revealed only to my mother, was to be a great rudimental drummer. My mother's stock reply was: "That's nice, Mickey. But how are you going to live? There's no money in rudimental drumming."

My options, if I were truly serious about becoming a professional drummer, were limited to orchestral, Big Band, jazz, or rock and roll. The orchestra was out of the question. I couldn't see myself sitting up there in a tuxedo

WHEN I WAS *learning to play my first drum set in the 1950s, Gene Krupa (below) and Buddy Rich were my particular heroes.*

crashing the cymbals together every ten minutes. I could, however, see myself as a Big Band drummer, like Krupa and Rich, except that the Big Bands had seen their day. By the early sixties only a few magnificent dinosaurs, like the Count Basie band and Duke Ellington, were left.

This wasn't the case with jazz. Jazz was still potent and healthy, but the style of drumming that had become predominant in the fifties, with its soft, brushwork groove, didn't feed my appetite for noise. So perhaps it was natural that I would gravitate to rock and roll. It was the latest extension of the African backbeat, the grandchild of the New Orleans sound that had fanned out to Memphis, the Delta, St. Louis, and up the river to Chicago, then spread via the phonograph, getting louder and louder as the century progressed, until it began to feed back into itself through amplified electrical instruments that magnified it a hundredfold. Elvis, Little Richard, Buddy Holly, Chuck Berry, the Big Bopper – I used to lug a phonograph out to the porch and beat along to the Hit Parade.

Rock and roll was hot, but among my friends it was not the most exciting thing around. The hot music was Latin, up from Cuba and the rest of the Caribbean – the mambo, the limbo, all those blaring trombones booming out over intricate pounding percussion played on African drums and rattles that had been virtually eliminated from the slave populations of the United States — congas, maracas, timbales, guiros. I remember screaming on the dance floor at the Colgate Gardens, the after-hours Latin club that Brian Burke first took me to. First the jacket would go, then the tie, then the top buttons of the shirt. After the first twenty minutes everyone was soaked with sweat. People were taking their clothes off, going crazy, and dancing for hours and hours. You could try out all sorts of emotions with the mambo; you didn't have to be that great a dancer. The *mambo* – there might have been one or two sweaty dancers at Colgate Gardens who could have paused in their gyrations to explain that a mambo was a vôdun priestess, but I never ran into one.

When I was sixteen I took a job as a soda jerk at a club in Atlantic Beach, Long Island, that hosted Latin bands. That's where I first saw Tito Puente. One of his percussionists would sometimes let me hang out in the back of the band, vamping on maracas or guiros. I used to watch the drummer's hands, trying to memorize how they manipulated the rhythm.

At the end of my junior year I finally beat Brian Burke for the first and only time before he graduated, appropriating the first chair in the percussion section. Midway through my senior year I succeeded him as first chair in the

Portrait of a Rudimental Drummer

All-State band, winning the competition with my father's snakewood sticks. Then, to my mother's horror, I quit high school and joined the air force.

I felt I had gone as far as I could as a kid drummer and was burning to test myself in the world of grown-up drummers. I wanted to become an adult as fast as possible, and the quickest way to accomplish that when I was young was the military.

They shaved my head and sent me to Lackland Air Force Base outside of San Antonio, Texas. I remember a cold rainy day my first week of basic training. I was looking out a window and crying, because all week long people had been sticking their face into mine and yelling at me, telling me they owned my ass. I was miserable. I remember thinking, "Get ahold of yourself. Millions of people have done this and survived."

One day I was in the base music room, packing up some drums, when I noticed a yellowed pamphlet in the bottom of one of the cases. It was an old advertising brochure for Remo Drumheads. Idly I turned the pages. And there he was, the tall, blonde drum god.

"Hi, I'm Lenny Hart. I've tried them all, and Remo WeatherKings are the finest."

CHAPTER FIVE

THE CIRCLE OF THE DRUM

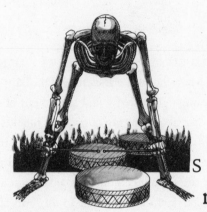

S A ROCK AND roll drummer, I'm the product of a collision between two percussive traditions. One is an oral tradition that came over from Africa, entering my bloodstream as a mute force that made me want to dance, dance, dance; the other tradition, which exists within the framework of Western musical history, fills whole walls in major research libraries with books about the piano, the violin, and even a few about the drum.

What saddens me now, as I remember that kid drummer who was burning to test himself in the world of men drummers, was how completely ignorant I was of my tradition – any tradition. An eight-year-old Minianka

67

hanging around the drum huts in his West African village knows more about his tradition than I knew about mine. At least he knows the origin myth of his instrument; I couldn't have begun to tell you where mine came from. Oh, I knew a little about the beginnings of the drum set, because it was such a recent invention, and I was vaguely aware that drummers during the American Revolution had needed a set of signals distinct from the British, starting a process that would culminate in the formal alphabet of the twenty-six American rudiments. But that was it. Nobody, no drummer, no teacher, no wise parent ever took me aside and said, "Mickey, in the beginning . . ."

"IN THE BEGINNING" IS A DANGEROUS THING TO SAY TO A MAN BUILDing a Timeline. It wasn't long before the one I was creating at the Barn stretched all the way back to the big bang, to that seed sound at the heart of creation. I had pegboards filled with data about our evolution from monkey to tool-wielding hominid. In terms of my quest, though, the story really begins about forty thousand years ago, when the primate *Homo sapiens* experienced a cultural explosion – our tools became elegant, our communities grew larger and more complex, and we began to make a record of our life in the form of painted images, brilliant portrayals of our emerging sensibilities, revealing a creature with an already highly developed sense of the sacred.

Very early on we began a dialogue with those invisible superior forces – the spirit world – that seemed to govern our lives. The sacred was something we did, like hunting and procreating; the way we approached it was through ritual.

As toolmakers we were busy striking, scraping, rubbing, shaking, swinging – verbs that perfectly describe the class of percussion instruments known as idiophones. The bodily rhythms and the percussive payoff are similar; only the context separates the striking of two flints to make a spearhead from the whacking of two sticks to make a rhythm.

Rhythm and noise. There is terror in noise, and in that terror there is also power.

One of the first things we did with this power to manipulate noise rhythmically was to use it in our sacred dance. Accompanying our sacred songs was sacred noise, rhythms created from the sounds found in the materials we

AROUND
15,000 B.C., an
anonymous artist
painted our first known
picture of a musician —
a man wearing the skin
of a dead animal and
playing some kind of
instrument, possibly a
sounding bow or a
concussion stick.

had at hand – wood, bone, stone, animal skin, assorted gourds and pods, plus the human body itself, which scholars like Blades and Sachs generally assumed was one of the very first instruments.

We clapped our hands and sang our sacred songs, which were probably simple vocalized syllables like *AhhhhhhhNaaaaaaahhhhhhh* or *Baaaaaaaaddddddinnnnnn,* but of powerful effect. I believe it was Joseph Campbell who steered me toward this description of the body percussion of the !Kung, a tribe of San (often called Bushmen) in Africa, a people who have only a few musical instruments: "The clapping and stamping are of such precision that they give the effect of a well-played battery of percussion instruments producing a solid structure of intricate rhythm. Above the percussion sounds, the voices of the men and women weave together in parts, singing the medicine songs. The curing dance draws people of a Bushmen band together into concerted action as nothing else does. They stamp and clap and sing with such precision that they become like an organic being. In this close configuration – together – they face the gods."

Sacred noise.

The common names we use for the succession of Stone Age periods – Paleolithic, Mesolithic, Neolithic – reflect the range and complexity of the tools made and used by the people of that time. So far, archaeologists excavating Paleolithic sites have found two types of sound makers: a few bone whistles and a lot of idiophones. A site in the Ukraine has turned up what might be a Stone Age percussionist's working kit: scrapers made out of mammoth jaws, beaters formed from reindeer antlers, plus a set of delicate wrist rattles, one of bone, the other made from seashells.

We have idiophones dating back to 20,000 B.C. that are daubed with red ochre, a decoration most scholars believe indicates a sacred usage. But the first "document" of percussion's connection with the sacred doesn't show up until the Middle Paleolithic, around 15,000 B.C., when an anonymous artist, working in a limestone cavern in southwestern France, painted our first known picture of a musician. Known as the dancing sorcerer (or shaman) of Les Trois Frères – a cave named for the three brothers who discovered it – this picture has been interpreted by scholars as representing a man wearing the skin of an animal and playing some kind of instrument, possibly a sounding bow or a concussion stick.

The dancing shaman of Les Trois Frères was painted at the climax of Paleolithic culture, when what Campbell in *The Way of the Animal Powers*

TIMELINE

*Dates are
approximate*

◆

**15 BILLION
YEARS AGO**

The big bang

◆

**3 BILLION
YEARS AGO**

Life begins on earth

◆

**450 MILLION
YEARS AGO**

First life on land

◆

**70 MILLION
YEARS AGO**

Rise of mammals

◆

**65 MILLION
YEARS AGO**

Dinosaurs die out

◆

**5–10 MILLION
YEARS AGO**

*Earliest
proto-hominids*

◆

**2,500,000
YEARS AGO**

Stones used as tools

◆

**1,600,000
YEARS AGO**

Crafted tools

400,000
YEARS AGO

Homo sapiens
appears

♦

60,000
YEARS AGO

*Development of
complex tools*

♦

50,000
YEARS AGO

*Humans first cross
land bridge from Asia
to North America
(last of these
migrations occurred
around 30,000
years ago)*

*Hunting bows,
musical bows*

*Earliest known
cave paintings*

♦

35,000
YEARS AGO

*Upper Paleolithic
period begins (through
10,000 years ago)*

*Idiophones (scrapers,
rattles, etc.)*

Bone flutes

♦

30,000
YEARS AGO

Cro-Magnon man

*Earliest goddess
iconography*

*Evidence of
shamanism*

calls "The Great Hunt" was still in full swing. The landscape of the European continent resembled today's Siberia, an immense semiglacial grassland over the surface of which migrated great herds of animals – bison, rhinoceros, mammoth – and our human ancestors. The generally accepted scenario has us living in small hunter-gatherer bands, following our main food source, summering in open air encampments and wintering in caves, where we left a wealth of puzzling documentation in the form of cave paintings, plus numerous other artifacts.

Campbell believed that the cave itself functioned as a kind of percussion instrument during sacred ceremonies. He thought that at certain moments in the ritual early percussionists would whack the stalactites, sending a resounding *boooong* echoing throughout the cavern. Joe told me that he had tested his hypothesis during one of his visits to the Paleolithic caves of Europe and that the resonant sound had left him even more convinced. An archaeological find in southern Russia lends weight to the theory that the cave itself was used as a resonating chamber. Excavating a small, semipermanent encampment, archaeologists uncovered a hut filled with idiophones and mammoth skulls. This was the community's sacred space – the village church – and unlike the other buildings, which were just frames over which skin had been stretched, this one was covered with earth, like an above-ground cave. The sod roof, theorized the archaeologists, was there for its acoustical properties.

Besides idiophones and flutes, we also began using an instrument known as a bullroarer. A bullroarer is a flat, elongated piece of bone or wood, attached at one end to a string that is swung over the head, lasso style, to produce a howl or a hum, depending on the instrument's shape and velocity. The first document of a bullroarer shows up, in the context of a death cult, on the wall of the vulture shrine in the Neolithic city of Çatal Hüyük, in southern Turkey.

Not too long after the painting of the dancing shaman of Les Trois Frères, the climate started to change. The glaciers began to melt. The weather, while not appreciably warmer, grew much wetter, causing the tundra to retreat to the east. The great herds followed, and some – the mammoth, the wooly rhinoceros – failed to adapt. Some of us also followed the Great Hunt, a few actually pushing across the Bering connector and down into the Americas before the waters from the melting glacial ice cap split the two continents. Others adapted to the immense forest that grew in place of the tundra. The Paleolithic gave way to the Mesolithic.

Scholars date the Mesolithic from about 10,000 B.C. to about 2700 B.C. in western Europe, although it was much shorter in the south and the Near East. Archaeological evidence gives us the first signs of the domestication of plants, a practice that began diffusing around 8000 B.C., spreading rapidly, until by 7000 B.C. we find the first flourishing of agriculture and the domestication of animals, principally sheep, goats, and cattle – the emergence of the Neolithic.

We have to wait until the Neolithic for the first evidence of membranophones – drums with skin heads. Just when the first drums were made is unknown, but at some point between the Paleolithic and the Neolithic, some genius discovered the exquisite percussive potential of skin, and, along with the domestication of animals, it diffused rapidly. In my more fanciful moments, I like to imagine that this was a case of what is known as "spontaneous diffusion." All over the planet, future drummers – members of Remo's one percent – went to sleep one night and dreamed the same dream of a tree body with an animal skin mouth – the wooden drum.

Towns appear for the first time in the Neolithic. Perhaps the best known is Çatal Hüyük. At its height, around 4500 B.C., Çatal Hüyük supported a population of close to six thousand people. Its main business was the sacred. It was a temple town, a pilgrimage spot like latter-day Mecca or Benares. Farmers, hunters, and herders of the outlying lands must have come here regularly to renew their connection with the sacred, worshiping at temples devoted to, among many others, the bull cult, the vulture cult, the bird cult, and the snake cult.

These have been called the gods and goddesses of Old Europe – multiple manifestations of one principle, known by such names as the great goddess, the great mother, the mother goddess, a society focused around fertility and the rhythmical attunement to nature that agriculture demands. James Mellaart, the principal excavator of Çatal Hüyük, reports that though men and women appeared to be about equal in status at Çatal Hüyük, the women did seem to run the religious and artistic side of life, while men handled the material side. Although much excavation still needs to be done on Neolithic sites, as a rule these goddess-worshiping agricultural societies seem to have been remarkably pacific.

A contemporary German scholar, Doris Stockmann, suggests that what went on in the sacred spaces of Çatal Hüyük were audiovisual dance rituals, where "each individual could experience and feel the event with all of

25,000
YEARS AGO
*Peak of mother goddess
and fertility beliefs*

20,000
YEARS AGO
Red ochre idiophones

15,000 B.C.
*The dancing shaman
of Les Trois Frères*

11,000 B.C.
*Last great ice age
(to 8,000 B.C.)*

10,000 B.C.
*Mesolithic period
(to 2700 B.C.)*

8000 B.C.
*Neolithic period
(to 3500 B.C.)*

*First Fertile Crescent
settlements*

*Domestication
of plants*

*Skin-covered drums
(membranophones)*

7000 B.C.
*Agriculture
flourishing in
Near East*

*Domestication
of animals*

his senses." Percussion was the driving musical force behind those rituals. Painted on the walls of Çatal Hüyük are images of concussion sticks and clappers, bullroarers and flutes. Numerous round stone cylinders with scooped-out ends have been found, leading Stockmann to speculate that they might have been drums whose skin heads had long ago decomposed.

According to archaeologist Marija Gimbutas, author of *The Language of the Goddess* and one of the major scholars attempting to reconstruct the consciousness of Neolithic Old Europe, there was "an intimate relationship between the drum and the goddess." The exact nature of that "intimate relationship" is still speculative, but there are some interesting points of departure, particularly a set of small clay ritual objects that were dug up in Bulgaria and date to about 4500 B.C. Gimbutas speculates that these miniatures, which include several altar stands, bowls, figurines, and drums, may be replicas of the actual objects used in the rituals performed for the bird goddess — the goddess of music. The three cylinder drums included in this set look just like congas, the classic wooden drums. In the Neolithic we also find the hourglass shape that gives us, at one extreme, the South Asian *damaru,* and, at the other, the talking drum of West Africa.

WESTERN CIVILIZATION IS GENERALLY THOUGHT TO HAVE BEGUN A few thousand years after the days of the bird goddess rituals in Çatal Hüyük. The origin of the modern, civilized world is generally dated from the third millennium B.C., and its emergence is usually located first in the brick city states of the Tigris and Euphrates watershed and then across the Mediterranean in the Nile valley of Egypt.

Our sense of the sacred shifted to the sky. During the Great Hunt, we found the sacred in the wandering rhythms of the herds (the way of the animal powers). With the rise of agriculture the sacred shifted to the seeded earth and its cycles of vegetative growth and decay. Now, with the so-called dawn of civilization, the sacred manifested itself in the rhythms of the stars and planetary bodies — the male sky gods. The new temple towns were even bigger than Çatal Hüyük. In the Fertile Crescent between the Tigris and Euphrates the river

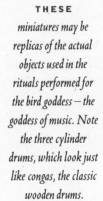

THESE miniatures may be replicas of the actual objects used in the rituals performed for the bird goddess — the goddess of music. Note the three cylinder drums, which look just like congas, the classic wooden drums.

1200 B.C.
*Rise of Dionysian
religion*

❖

1100 B.C.
*Bronze drums in
China*

❖

1000 B.C.
*Large-scale slash-and-
burn agriculture*

*Kettledrums in
Babylonia and India*

❖

800 B.C.
*Rise of Apollonian
religion*

❖

700 B.C.
Drums in Babylonia

❖

600 B.C.
Rise of Hinduism

❖

628–551 B.C.
Zoroaster

❖

623–543 B.C.
Buddha

❖

551–479 B.C.
Confucius

❖

470–399 B.C.
Socrates

towns of Ur, Kish, and Uruk flourished in what is known as the Sumerian civilization. In terms of the sacred, Sumer lies at the cultural crossroads between the declining mother goddess ethos of the Neolithic, and the rise of the male sky gods, who responded to their predecessor by converting her most sacred symbols — the snake, the bull, the naked female body — into their most feared ones.

The sacred songs were chanted daily in the temples, an event of such importance that the larger temples maintained their own music schools, which just may be the oldest institutes of higher education we know about. Besides instruction in the singing of the songs, these schools were also increasingly involved in the teaching of instruments. There had been a revolution in instrumentation since the Neolithic: harps and the first horns were added to the orchestra of clappers, rattles, flutes, and drums.

Sacred noise gave way to sacred music, and the result was an explosion of song. One of the most fascinating things archaeologists have uncovered is a sort of Sumerian hit parade, which lists a wide variety of song types: religious songs, work songs, songs of victory and heroism, songs praising the royal family, and love songs. This was the singing world of the Old Testament. The land was sparsely dotted with villages; the surrounding hills were populated by farmers and shepherds and nomads, with caravan tracks disappearing off the edge of the map — toward Egypt, toward India, toward Africa. Every so often a city appeared, a humming urban hive of wealth and power, both spiritual and temporal. Even back then the very rich, to say nothing of the royalty, were different from you and me. When the Jewish patriarch Abraham lived in Hebron — he was born in Ur — he had 318 servants. And probably a couple of them were drummers — temple drummers by day, street drummers by night — playing huge Sumerian frame drums.

The first images of drums we find date to around 2200 B.C. and show mainly frame drums, both round and square. I must have glanced at these pictures dozens of times, before I began noticing how many of antiquity's drummers were women — certainly half, maybe more. The classic frame drum image that turned up everywhere showed a couple of Bacchantes — wild Greek dancing women, their hair flying in their dance as they beat on a frame drum. I also discovered that the first drummer whose name we actually know was a woman, the granddaughter of the Sumerian king. She lived in Ur in 2280 B.C., and played the *balag-di* in the temple of the moon, one of the mother goddess's strongest symbols.

THIS WAS
*the singing world of the
Old Testament.*

In some sense all Western drummers are descended from this woman, an irony I could appreciate, since by the time I came along the drum was a militantly male instrument, and had been for hundreds if not thousands of years. Women just didn't drum; my mother was a rare exception to that rule.

I was so excited by these early images of Sumerian frame drums that for a long time I didn't notice what was happening: as sacred music replaced sacred noise, the drum was falling to the side, losing rank as it came toward me in history. The trumpet, harp, lyre, and shawm — the angelic sounds of these instruments were prospering in this newly civilized world, but not the drum. An examination of Assyrian bas-reliefs reveals a preference for stringed instruments. The favored instruments of the Jews were the trumpet and the harp. One of the few places you find real drumming in the Old Testament is after the parting of the Red Sea, when "Miriam, the prophetess, the sister of Aaron, took a timbrel in her hand; and all the women went out after her with timbrels and with dances." With the adoption of Christianity by the Roman Empire, wrote Blades, percussive music was banned as "mischievous" and "licentious"; the drum and cymbals were particularly singled out as evidence of "the devil's pomposity."

Although you do find on ancient frescoes an occasional kettledrum or goblet drum, and the use of rattles continues unabated, the Neolithic congas and the African-looking hourglass drums seem to have disappeared, leaving the frame drum as the most prominent drum of the ancient world. (Bend a thin, tensile slice of wood into a hoop and affix skin to one side. You have made the classic drum of the Western percussive tradition. It went by many names — the *duff, toff, tambour, timbrel, dampha, bendair, tambattam, tumbuttu, tympanum, tar*.) In some sense, as B.C. becomes A.D., we reach a zero point in the written history and in the archaeology of the drum in the West, and it will take the next eighteen hundred years for the drum to make a slow recovery, usually with the help of cultures that were not Western.

KICKED OUT OF THE TEMPLE, THE DRUM FOUND A PLACE ON THE battlefield. The history of the drum in the West is dominated by the history of the war drum, as the drum's ability to manipulate noise into rhythm came to be valued for its martial rather than its magical power. Drums provided the music of war, and the favored war drum was the kettledrum, whose terrible low booming could be heard for miles. Often of immense size, these kettledrums were carried into battle, strapped to horses and camels or dragged behind in carts. There are kettledrums from ancient India, from the time of the ancient holy text, the *Mahabharata,* that measure five feet in diameter and weigh approximately four hundred and fifty pounds. You needed an elephant to lug them around. "There arose a tumultuous uproar caused by the blare of the trumpet and the thundering of drums, the blowing of conch shells," says the *Mahabharata.* "The very sky was rent by the beating of drums."

Drums were the driving force behind the percussive din that permeated the ancient art of war. The name of the game was to energize your troops while terrifying your enemies with the heroic quality of the noise you could make. The Egyptians massed their drummers in the center of their attack. Trumpets were used for communication between units; the drums were there solely to get the adrenaline flowing.

But then the war drum also faded from the Western tradition. The European armies in the Middle Ages preferred the flute on the battlefield. It would be a thousand years before Western Christian ears heard the din of battle as it had been known in ancient days, and it scared the armor off them when they heard it. It happened during the First Crusade, when the Christian knights met the Saracen armies for the first time in Palestine. What shocked them most, much more than the Saracen swords, was the noise these Muslims made — with trumpets, drums, cymbals, pipes — as they rode into battle. "They did this," wrote one chronicler, "to excite their spirit and courage, for the more violent the clamor became, the more bold they were for the frey." As long as the drums pounded, the Saracens fought fiercely. But when the drums fell silent, the Saracen will to fight flagged. It meant that the drums had been taken, which was the equivalent of the Christian concept of losing your colors.

Once they got over their terror of this music made by heathens, the Christians immediately adopted their instruments, particularly the kettledrum. Over the next few centuries, military conflicts with the Ottoman Empire stimulated a percussive revival in Europe. Blades gave me the litany: the barrel drum arrived in the twelfth century, followed two centuries later by the sidedrum, frequently with snares attached, and a few centuries after that the bass drum. Almost as soon as it arrived in the eighteenth century, composers like Gluck,

356–323 B.C.
Alexander the Great

♦

204 B.C.
*Anatolian Cybele
shrine in Temple of
Victory at Rome*

♦

4 B.C.
*Birth of Christ;
Christian era begins*

♦

570–632 A.D.
*Muhammad
(rise of Islam)*

♦

900
*Viking settlements in
North America*

♦

1095
First Crusade

♦

1100
*Barrel drum
introduced in Europe*

♦

1300
*Side drum introduced
in Europe*

*Turkish Janissary
bands (abolished
in 1826)*

♦

1492
*Columbus lands in
North America*

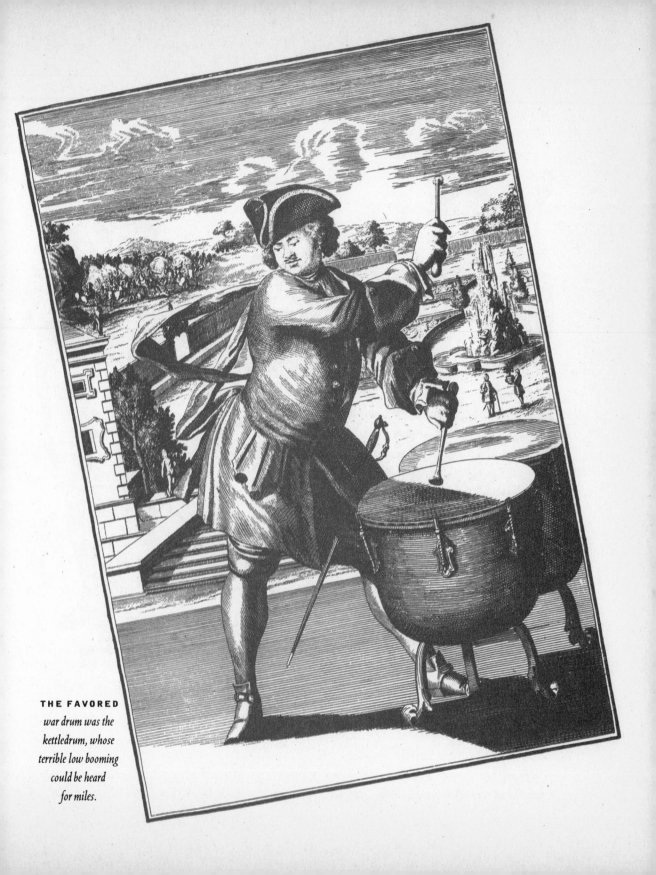

THE FAVORED *war drum was the kettledrum, whose terrible low booming could be heard for miles.*

THE MILITARY
preserved the art of the
din and nurtured the
brotherhood of the
drum in our culture.

Mozart, and Beethoven began experimenting with the bass drum's orchestral possibilities, often using it as a way of reinforcing a musical peak experience.

It wasn't easy for the drum to get reinstated in Western music. Blades quotes a sixteenth-century membranophobe who was not at all pleased with the reappearance of these big loud drums: "They cause much unrest to pious old people of the earth, to the sick and weakly, the devout in the cloisters, those who have read, studied and prayed, and I verily believe that the devil must have had the devising and making of them, for there is no pleasure or anything good about them. If hammering and raising a din be music, then coopers and those who make barrels must be musicians."

The military preserved the art of the din and nurtured the brotherhood of the drum in our culture. By the time of the Renaissance, the armies of Europe were beginning to work out supple musical languages that would allow them to communicate group information during the battle. The trumpet was the voice of the cavalry, while the drum belonged to the infantry. The ears of the horse soldiers were attuned to a variety of signals — saddle, mount, mess, march, alarm, charge — while those of the footsoldier listened for changes in rhythm that indicated such things as march, alarm, approach, assault, battle, retreat, skirmish. Drummers held a privileged position on the field of battle. It was considered dishonorable to strike or wound a drummer, although capturing a foe's drums was still a glorious moment. In fact, capturing a drum was the only way many regiments obtained some of the more valuable military drums. In England, only the Royal Irish Dragoons and the King's Dragoons were allowed to have kettledrums, and then only one apiece. In the German army, kettledrums were reserved for those regiments led by noblemen.

The Germans were generally considered the vanguard when it came to military music. They drew their musicians from an ancient guild known as the Royal Trumpeters and Army Kettle Drummers. Exempt from military law and with their own tribunals to punish offenders, guild musicians were in intense demand. The Russian monarch Peter the Great had his own personal regimental band of Germans, as did the king of Portugal.

Drummers were paid a princely wage, five shillings a day, and in return they were expected to be a cut above the usual recruit. According to Grose's *Military Antiquities* (published in 1801), drummers needed to be "faithful, secret and ingenious, of able personage to use their instruments, and office of sundry languages. For often times they be sent to parlay with their enemy, to summon their forts or towns, to redeem and conduct prisoners, and diverse other messages which of necessity require language. If such drums and fifes should fortune to fall into the hands of the enemies, no gift nor force should cause them to disclose any secrets that they know."

In the middle of the eighteenth century the royal houses of Europe, especially those of the Austro-Hungarian empire, were once again confronted by a rising power to the East: the Ottoman Empire. The Turks had been expanding their sovereign territory since the fifteenth century, aided by the first full-time professional army, called the Janissaries, who marched and fought to a beat laid down by shawms, fife, kettledrums, tenor drums, and a big bass drum, with a couple of cymbals and triangles thrown in for color. This noise was irresistible; within several decades every European army, with the exception of England's, was marching to the strains of Turkish percussion.

When the American Revolution broke out in 1775, the drummers of the Continental army employed the drum signals of the rival British, only gradually evolving the distinctive style that has been shaped and codified until, in this century, it became the twenty-six rudiments that I spent my adolescence trying to master.

CHAPTER SIX

Portrait Of A Drummer As A Cold Warrior

T WAS THE HEIGHT OF the Cold War when I enlisted in the air force. Kennedy and Krushchev were nose to nose, and it really did seem possible that the world might end tomorrow. Even if somebody had built a kettledrum as big as a football field, it wouldn't have begun to compare to the terror-evoking potential of a jet engine screaming on the runway. Yet the military still had a role for drummers. Every evening I would strap on my instrument and drum retreat, quick-marching several hundred men for several miles

83

across March Air Force Base, outside Riverside, in Southern California, where I'd been posted after basic training.

I rented a car my first free weekend and drove to Los Angeles to search for the North Hollywood location of Remo Weatherking Drumheads. Remo Belli was a legend in the percussion industry, having invented the plastic drumhead, which freed drummers from the eccentricities of skin, allowing us to play in all kinds of weather. I remember him walking toward me across the factory floor, which was filled with thousands of his drumheads, a small, regal man who grasped my hand and said, "Michael, I haven't seen you since you were a baby."

For a second, everything spun. This man had seen me as a baby? That implied that my father had still been around after my birth. That implied . . . but the implications were not what I had come for; they could wait. What I most wanted Remo surprisingly provided. After years of no contact, he'd recently run into Lenny Hart. My father, he said, had an executive position in a savings and loan out in the valley. *My father was a banker?*

I suspect Remo called him. In any case Lenny didn't seem surprised when his secretary announced that a Michael Hart was there to see him. He got up from behind his gleaming banker's desk when I entered the room and came around to shake my hand. Physically he was my exact opposite: six feet tall, blonde, and weighing two hundred plus pounds, which he carried well since he played handball often. His manner suggested he'd decided to endure whatever was about to happen with amused dignity.

I don't know what Lenny thought I was going to do, but he can't have expected me to pull out the snakewood sticks he'd won so long ago and hand them to him. All my life I had heard about my father's famous long roll, played in what was called the Ancient Corps style of 110 beats per minute. This technique had died out after the war; Lenny was one of the last masters who could drum the rudiments at this speed.

I asked him to play something at the old speed. He picked up the sticks and then, very slowly and elegantly, he began to tap out a famous rudimental solo called "The Downfall of Paris." Ten minutes later we were grabbing our coats and dashing for the nearest music store to buy a second pair of sticks. We spent the rest of the afternoon in his office drumming on desks, phone books, chairs — I had met the drum god at last, and he was a wonderful guy, fun loving, generous, witty, and despite years of inactivity still a brilliant drummer.

My next posting was to a Strategic Air Command base outside of Madrid, and we promised to keep in touch while I was in Spain. But a few months after I arrived Lenny vanished again. His phone was disconnected; my letters came back stamped "addressee unknown."

MY MUSICAL DUTIES IN SPAIN WERE MORE VARIED THAN THEY HAD been at Riverside. A lot of my time in the early months was spent crammed into an aging tour bus with thirty-five other guys, our instruments roped to the roof, driving up and down twisty narrow roads at speeds approaching twenty miles per hour, bringing culture to the lovely ancient towns of Iberia.

As the town came to life in the morning, there we'd be — the best marching band anyone could expect after seventeen hours on a cramped bus, swinging smartly by, blaring out the war songs of the greatest military power on the planet. The Spaniards were always slightly stunned before they caught on.

"Estan los GIs norteamericanos!"

At night we transformed ourselves into a different kind of ambassador, becoming a tight sixteen-piece dance band, laying down Duke Ellington, Glenn Miller, Count Basie. Everyone came, the mayor, the town kids, peasants, and shepherds who lived a half day's walk away in the hills. It was a true festival. Afterward we would wander around the town, drinking wine, feeling young and a little wild, yet hearing somewhere in the back of our minds:

"You men are guests in another country, one that is not part of the free world."

Spain was so mesmerizing that it was necessary to remind yourself that it was also a fascist state run by a gestapo in funny hats. The *Guardia Civil* was Francisco Franco's private army. Fall into their hands and you might be tortured, maybe murdered, at least that's what the Pentagon wanted us to think. The American brass was so concerned that an "incident" not take place between the two armed groups that they'd installed special phones in all the bars and GI hangouts around the base. All a bartender had to do when a fight started was lift the receiver and the Air Police would be on the way.

I MET POGO MY FIRST DAY IN SPAIN. I HADN'T EVEN BEEN THERE TWO hours, arriving just in time for lunch. As a new guy I was quizzed by everyone at the table. "You got a girl, Hart? You play any sports, Hart?" I said I was into judo, which wasn't exactly untrue, since I'd messed around with it back on the base in California. But I lied when someone asked me what belt I was, telling them, "Brown." And when this same person asked what my favorite throw was, I just made one up. I was so excited to be out of America, in uniform, and hanging out with the guys that I didn't think twice about stretching the truth.

As I rose to leave someone handed me a note. "Pogo wanted to be sure you got this."

The note said: "Be prepared to defend your belt at four o'clock tomorrow. Or else you are a dead man."

Pogo, it turned out, was the name of the solid-looking guy who had asked me what belt I was. He was base judo instructor. In fact he was European champion in the 160-pound weight class. And he was crazy. Just how crazy I was to learn that evening. As news of my predicament spread, an alarming number of people sought me out to tell me horrible Pogo stories. Everyone was terrified of him and all agreed I should treat that second sentence in his note quite literally.

I had two options, it seemed to me. I could skip the meeting and the beating and try to avoid Pogo for the rest of my days on the base, which was unlikely to happen. Or, I could keep the appointment and humbly throw myself upon his reportedly nonexistent mercy. I decided to keep the appointment and rely on charm and groveling.

I had diarrhea all morning. I still remember the whine the gym door made as it swung open. I hadn't bothered to change into gym clothes, thinking that would be needlessly provocative. I was wearing fatigues. So was Pogo. He was leaning against a locker, looking like an overmuscled tree stump with a deceptive baby face. When he saw me he smiled.

"I was only bragging to the guys about being a brown belt," I began. "That was stupid, I know that. You can either beat the shit out of me, which Lord knows I deserve, or you can teach me judo, become my teacher, that's what I really want. I'm so stupid it wouldn't be any fun to beat me up."

THERE WE'D *be — the best marching band anyone could expect after seventeen hours on a cramped bus.*

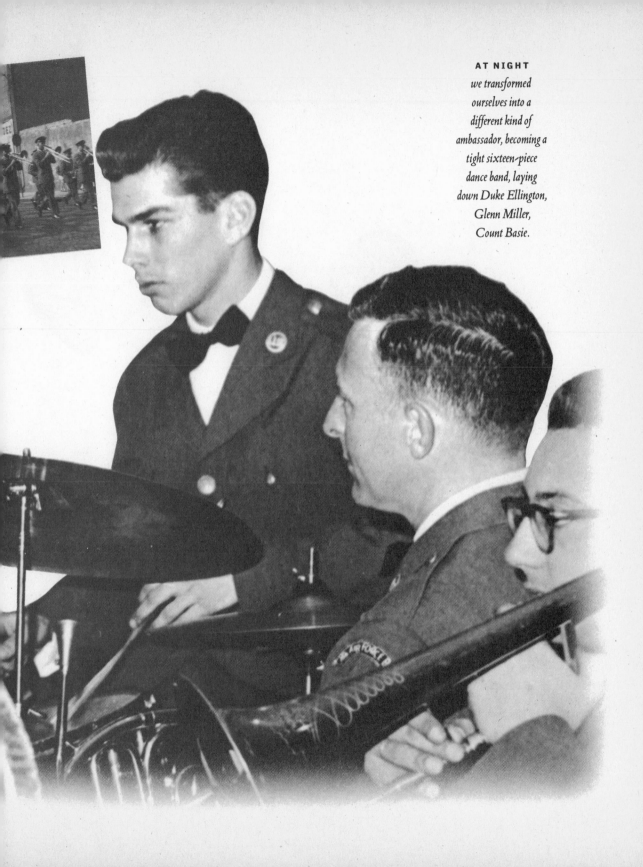

AT NIGHT
*we transformed
ourselves into a
different kind of
ambassador, becoming a
tight sixteen-piece
dance band, laying
down Duke Ellington,
Glenn Miller,
Count Basie.*

"YOU FALL *real good," he said.*

Pogo had a soft, calm voice. "Shut up," he said. "Let's step into the dojo and see what you can do."

It seemed to go on for five or six hours, though it probably took only ten minutes. I spent most of the time upside down, Pogo tossing me around like a rag doll. Not maliciously. He didn't slam me to the mat or anything like that. In fact, he rather gently broke my falls, but he seemed to be doing it to keep me conscious longer, so he could go on tossing me.

"You fall real good," he said.

After he stopped I lay gasping on the mat, concussed, bruised, everything spinning.

"Be here tomorrow at two, unless you're too weak to make it."

As I would soon learn, Pogo had made a special study of the weakness/strength continuum. It was his one area of personal philosophy. I would also learn that Pogo had a dream of sweeping the European armed forces judo championships. He already was coaching the superheavyweight and the heavyweight champions, and he himself owned the middleweight. What he needed was someone in the 130-and-under class – me. The Spain and Morocco tournaments were nine months away, when Pogo, after my third or fourth lesson, made his proposition: "You could be champion. You don't realize it, but in a year you could be European champ. I could make you a winner. I know what it takes, and you could do it. The only thing stopping you would be your own weakness."

Champion! What eighteen-year-old male doesn't love the taste of that word?

Every spare moment after that was spent working out, lifting weights, sparring. When Pogo decided that band was taking too much of my time, he had me reassigned as his personal assistant. This was a relief since it meant I no longer had to go on those awful band trips. I hated the pompous captain in charge. Pogo rescued me from this nonsense. He became my first teacher, in the higher sense. For the first time in my life I allowed myself to be absorbed by another's will. I was like a dog on a leash, and I didn't care, because Pogo was teaching me such incredible things. I belonged to him.

I became a guinea pig for all the techniques he had dreamed up over the years but hadn't dared try. He'd throw me for hours; he'd have me stare into his eyes, telling me, "Always watch your opponent's eyes. That's the quickest way to find out who he is and what he's going to do." Then he'd blindfold me and toss me some more, teaching me to maintain my balance while being propelled through the air. Leaving the blindfold on, he'd begin attacking. "Try to feel my thought," he'd say. "Learn how to sense with your body, not just your mind. Learn to read the movements of air a rushing body makes."

Even when I was asleep, Pogo remained my teacher. "If you're going to win the championship," he told me, "you can't afford to waste eight hours a night dreaming frivolous dreams. From now on, whenever you dream, I'm going to be there attacking you." And he was. As soon as my head hit the pillow the attacks would begin, continuing all night.

Pogo taught me how to get into a zone of complete focus, a physical room that I could enter in my head. I'd sit in there, waiting for my match to begin, building energy. When I hit the mat there was almost an audible explosion, yet I felt completely calm and in control.

Have you ever looked into a tiger's eye? What immediately grips you is that the tiger is right there — all four hundred and fifty pounds focused with gleaming maximum attention on you. No distractions, no hesitations, just a calm powerful contemplation. For thirty years the "eye of the tiger" focusing technique has been my fundamental approach to life. It's what gives me my velocity. Focus attention. Choose a line of attack.

Pogo made me into a contest animal, like a greyhound or a fighting cock. He had me completely programmed to go out and kick ass. "People think you're crazy," he told me. "You're so intense when you fight you scare them. Their fear is a powerful weapon. Learn to use it."

That was my persona in the early matches: Pogo's psychotic white-belt killer. My first opponent in formal competition was a first-degree brown belt. The whole time before our match began I just stared at him, saying my tiger mantra over and over: "You're mine." Every time he looked over at me I was right there, intently watching his every move. He was so nervous by the time we got onto the mat that I easily caught him in a quick mistake and picked up the first point. The gym went crazy. It was my first taste of loud, personal applause. After I started winning, my persona changed. I became a disinterested Zen warrior. I would sit cross-legged on the edge of the mat, showing no interest in the matches taking place before me.

Pogo owned me for eighteen months, the longest, most intense, and strangest educational experience of my life. Just as he predicted, I won my weight class at the European championships. But then it was over. Pogo's tour was up, and he was rotated back to the States. The last I ever heard of him was a rumor several months later that he had punched out his new commanding officer and had been either sentenced to the brig or dishonorably discharged, or both. I never saw him again.

It was as if a spell had been broken, as if I had spent eighteen months in a dream world that was not entirely a dream because when I awoke I discovered I had a completely different body and a transformed mental attitude. I had the eye of the tiger, and for that I am eternally grateful to Pogo. For me, the process involves consciously attempting to master your energy flows – the body flow, the mind flow, and the higher flow, the spirit side. Its ideal – seldom realized – is to achieve a kind of perfect balance that allows you to place your attention and energy exactly where you want it.

I MOVED OFF BASE AFTER POGO LEFT, SHARING AN APARTMENT IN Madrid with a Venezuelan playboy who was one of the salesmen at the place where I had bought a used Alfa Romeo. Raphael Baez was one of the suavest guys I have ever met. The perfect host, his passion was throwing parties for Madrid's young jet-setters, and he knew more beautiful women than I had ever thought existed. I fit into the decor as one of his flamboyant gestures.

Just before enlisting I had discovered the music of Babatunde Olatunji, the Nigerian drummer who lives in New York. It was my first exposure to the mother rhythms from West Africa that later mutated into my tradition, becoming rock and roll. All I knew then was that whenever I played this music at one of Raphael's parties, the room would transform. It was as though the rhythm of the drum was calling up something from these sleek cosmopolitan bodies that had been asleep. There was a power here that I couldn't ignore. It was calling me back to the drum. When I think back on my years in Spain, the sight of Raphael's friends going wild to Olatunji still resonates in my mind and seems a more important part of the story now than it did then.

One leave I traveled across North Africa. In Morocco I stumbled into a village that was celebrating the hashish harvest. The drumming had been going on for days, accompanied by big, loud double-reed pipes. Everyone was smoking hash. In the square, dervishes danced themselves into trance, pushing thin, razor-sharp skewers through their cheeks. Someone told me that if the dancers felt pain, they weren't truly in trance.

I LEFT SPAIN, AND THE AIR FORCE, IN 1965. BACK IN NEW YORK I SET about becoming a professional drummer, which meant learning to deal with the musicians' union. The New York musicians' union wasn't like a regular union; it was more like a booking agency that had a closed-shop deal with the clubs.

Every Thursday, if you wanted a weekend gig, you had to go to the union hall, which was in the basement of Roseland, the famous ballroom in the West Fifties. Hundreds of guys would be there. Whoever needed to book a player would go up to the microphone and say something like, "I need a drummer for a St. Valentine's Day dance at a school in Hoboken." If you wanted the job, you jotted it down in your book. Hundreds of anxious musicians milled around hopefully, masking their anxiety with all kinds of weird trips — what did this have to do with music? For the first time I questioned my commitment to the drum. This was the life I had chosen for myself?

My first and only job with the union was filling in as a drummer in a fox-trot band that had a regular gig at an over-fifty club. Lots of clarinets and brushwork. The job had the potential of lasting several weeks, and, completed successfully, it would have been a major step in my union career, but unfortunately I got fired after the first weekend. I was just too young, too excitable, too loud. I couldn't fit into their groove. I kept trying to rock.

Out of the blue a letter arrived from my father. Without mentioning where he'd been, he wrote that he was opening a music store in the town of San Carlos, near San Francisco. Would I like to join him in the business? I packed my stuff and moved west.

All Lenny had for stock was a couple of drums and a whole lot of cheap Japanese guitars. "Dad," I said, "this is a guitar store. We should be a drum store." I had a vision of turning this little space into the best drum hut in Northern California — wall-to-wall drums, drums hanging from the ceiling, people having to walk around dozens of drums before they could get to the counter. Within a few weeks we had changed our name from Hart Music to Drum City.

It was a smart time to get into the percussion business, since the back-beat was exploding up through rock and roll and out into the marketplace in the form of thousands of garage bands. Our cheapest drum sets were within the range of a middle-class parent who was resigned to appeasing junior's desire to be Ringo Starr. We sold hundreds.

Life was pretty easy in the music retail business. The mornings were usually dead. I set up a little shop in the back of the store and learned how to retool old drums. Most mornings I worked in the shop and then spent a few hours drumming on my pad, practicing the old rudimental solos my father used to play, learning them from books he'd loaned me. This was all I did for two years.

Lenny and I had a complex yet incredibly simple relationship. I was his son, of course, but it would be emotionally truer to say that I was more like his junior partner and number-one employee. The only intimate times we shared were when we became master and student and Lenny showed me what he knew of the old techniques. Whenever the opportunity presented itself, I pressed him to drum with me. At night we'd stand at the glass counter and drum on our pads in perfect unison for hours, often attracting a crowd.

Lenny liked to reminisce about the old days. He told me how in the early corps you had to practice in big mirrored rooms, using pads. That way you could synchronize every arm movement. You would do this for hundreds of hours, after work and on weekends. It became a male ritual; people got consumed by it. Some would quit their jobs and drum all day — "drum bums," Lenny called them. The way he described the early corps, they sounded like rival street gangs who brawled with drums, valve bugles, and cymbals instead of knives and guns.

The one topic we carefully avoided was why he had left. As near as I could piece it together, after leaving New York in the forties, Lenny had gone to Los Angeles, where he pioneered the West Coast drum and bugle scene. His forte was a series of intricate field maneuvers using flags and color guards, eight steps to the left, then ten forward, then fifteen to the right — that sort of stuff. He'd spend all day making diagrams of routines he saw in his head.

Once a week Lenny flew down to to Los Angeles to drill the girls at one of the Maryknoll high schools, and after a while he began bringing me along to help with the drumming. For three years running, these Japanese-American girls had won the California state championship in their class. There were eighty or ninety of them — all in their early teens — and some days they became an eighty-headed beast of rhythm and noise. At the state championship in 1965, a contingent of them came skipping up to Lenny and me.

THE GUY'S
*name was Billy
Kreutzmann.*

"Oh, Mr. Hart, sirs," they giggled. "We have entered you both in the solo rudimental championship." My heart fell. The last thing I wanted to do was compete against Lenny. He was so much better than I was, his technique so much finer.

Drum corps competitions take place during the day and the evening is given over to the lengthy award ceremonies. I remember hearing them call last place, then third place, then second. "Hart," the announcer said. I started to walk forward. "Leonard." I stopped where I was and looked over at Lenny, who was on the other side of the corps. He was looking at me, his face a mask. Then he smiled and went to collect his trophy.

"Hart, Michael."

I think something changed in me from that day forward, or was it in him? Lenny was still the same charming, roguish guy, but there was an edge to our interactions that hadn't been there before.

WE USED TO OFFER DRUM CLINICS AT THE STORE WITH BIG-NAME drummers, if we could get them. The biggest name we had was Sonny Payne, who was Count Basie's drummer. Sonny had consummate chops, powering the Basie band with a kind of smooth, easy energy that can't be learned — you're born with it; it's a function of temperament. He and I became friends, and we used to get together whenever Basie played San Francisco.

One night I was in the audience at one of Sonny's shows at the Fillmore when a friend introduced me to a drummer in a local band called the Grateful Dead. The guy's name was Billy Kreutzmann. I liked Kreutzmann immediately and after the gig we hung around outside drumming on cars and talking. Kreutzmann suggested we go hear some friends of his, a band called Big Brother and the Holding Company, which was playing at a club called the Matrix. I sent word backstage for Sonny to meet us there.

I had no idea what to expect, but I certainly wasn't prepared for the Matrix. It was like a big hallway that some lunatic entrepreneur had decided to turn into a music club. There was a plywood platform about six inches off the ground at one end — this was the stage. The place was full, and I was way in the back, but I stood up on a chair and could see this big crazed guitarist who looked like he was humping his amp.

The guy's name, I later learned, was James Gurley. He was rubbing his guitar against his amp, making it feed back like crazy. His guitar was barking out sounds I hadn't thought possible, huge spirals of noise that would twist around like a snake eating its tail. Then the whole band was feeding back. The din was incredible. And just as the noise was starting to get unbearable, up to the mike stepped a singer who opened her mouth and split my head with a thunderous cry. It was Janis Joplin.

I felt as if I'd fallen through a time warp into another universe. This incredible music had been happening just a few miles from where I was and I hadn't known anything about it! I was grinning so hard my jaws were starting to ache, and I was still grinning when Sonny arrived. He endured it for a few minutes, then leaned over to me and shouted, "This stuff is awful! I'm getting a headache."

There followed one of those classic moments as Sonny stood and prepared to leave and then noticed that I hadn't budged.

"I'm gonna stay a while longer. I think this stuff is amazing."

CHAPTER SEVEN

AMONG THE ETHNOS

JOSEPH CAMPBELL SAID that if you follow your bliss, doors open and guides appear, though probably not the ones you expect. That was certainly my experience at the Barn as I pursued my drum quest. I thought of my guides as dance partners.

Betsy Cohen was the first. One day I glanced up and there she was, frowning at the Timeline. A few minutes later this Ph.D. from Stanford, specialty in psychoacoustics, was critiquing my personality and pointing out obvious holes in what I had done. Life got louder and faster after Betsy arrived. Suddenly my phone was ringing at all hours. I thought I was an energy maniac — Betsy was like a horse that had been penned all winter. She was ready to gallop. Better still, she knew which way to run.

Betsy was a hard-headed scientist who loved detail, and one of the first things she brought to my quest was a rigid quality ethic. We wouldn't just go after myths, Betsy explained in her no-nonsense way; we'd go after the earliest transcriptions of those myths. Primary sources! Nothing but the facts! The second thing she brought to the project was cybernetics. She took us micro, into the computer world. One day she said to me, "We've been doing this all wrong. We should be entering everything into the big mainframe at Karma. I hate to say this, Mickey, but the Timeline's time has come."

We dismantled the Timeline, packed it into boxes, and drove south to the Stanford Center for Computer Research in Music and Acoustics. CCRMA – which everyone pronounced "Karma" – was housed in a complex of old buildings in the rolling farmlands outside of Stanford. It had once been the home of the artificial intelligence lab; it wasn't at all odd to run into a robot in the parking lot trailed by a couple of classic computer jockeys.

I was never exactly clear what story Betsy fed the Stanford authorities to explain our sudden and not exactly subtle presence at Karma. She was a distinguished scholar, of course, and as a member of the Grateful Dead I was not without a certain exotic legitimacy. Whatever the explanation, no one seemed bothered by the fact that two or three times a week we commandeered the mainframe, frequently filling every workstation with recruits who, for an honest wage, transformed my scrawled notes and underlined books into bits and bytes.

We would assemble around ten o'clock in the evening, when the building was nearly empty, and work into the morning. I'd glide from workstation to workstation, culling, watching, typing, reading over shoulders as the information was entered into the big computer:

When the anthropologist John Roscoe came to Banzanhole, he found, at a little distance from the royal kraal, a small enclosure in which stood the hut of the royal drums. The hut was always domed and had no point or pinnacle; inside there was a bed containing two drums. At the back of the hut, behind the bed, lay a quantity of material for repairing these drums and this had to be carefully guarded for it couldn't be used for any other purpose.

In front of the bed or stand was a row of pots belonging to the drums in which the daily offering of milk was put. The chief drums were the two that lay upon the bed. These were covered with white skins with a black strip making them look like a pair of great eyes in the gloom. A sacred herd of cows yielded a supply of milk that was daily offered to these drums in the pots that stood in front of them.

The milk was placed there in the morning and remained there until nine or ten o'clock at night, by which time the drum spirits would have drunk their fill and the rest could be swallowed by the drums' guardians. Beside the drum guardians, there was also a woman who was known as the wife of the drums, whose duty it was to look after the milk and the arrangement of the drums on the bed. Another woman looked after the fire in the drum house, which had to be kept burning at all times because the drums required warmth.

Offerings of beer and cattle were made to the drums by chiefs when a son had been born to them or when they had received promotion to some office or earned the commendation of the king. The king also made an annual offering of cows to the drums so that the drums possessed a large herd. Those cows offered to the first drum had to be red or white and those offered to the second drum had to be black. These cows were sacred. They provided the milk for the drums. Only the king could order one of these cows killed and only the guardians of the drums were allowed to eat the meat of the dead cow. The skin was kept for repairing the drums.

Our plan was to feed all the data we had into the computer and then categorize it as efficiently as possible. In the back of my mind I was hoping that a pattern would appear, but even if it didn't I felt I had made a quantum leap beyond the three-by-five-card technologies that scholars were still using.

I don't know when it dawned on me that the computer had taken the Timeline and mutated it into something marvelously strange, but gradually I began to feel that we were growing something almost organic in a new kind of reality, in cyberspace, growing it out of information. The Anaconda became a pulsing tree of data that I loved to climb around in, scanning for new growth.

MY FIRST DAY AT KARMA, BETSY HAD A SURPRISE FOR ME. SHE WANTED to introduce me to one of Karma's music moles.

You!

It was the guy who had picked up my *damaru* in the Barn.

Andy Schloss, as near as I could tell after I got to know him, was a professional student. He had studied mathematics and ethnomusicology, and he would be getting an advanced degree as soon as he finished writing up his data on the human perception of rhythm, which is what he'd been doing at Karma for the past few years. As I understood it, the research was pretty much complete; all that remained was the typing. But this kept getting postponed because Andy was always disappearing for weeks at a time to Cuba to record things like street festivals for Moe Asch's Folkways label.

This interested me because field recording was a passion of mine. I'd been running around with a Nagra (the first high-quality portable recorder) since the late sixties, taping whatever little pulses of world music passed through the Bay Area. I fantasized creating a network of demon tapers who at a moment's notice could run out and preserve whatever rare vibrations needed preserving. Listening to Schloss talk about what he did, I realized that there already was a network of demon tapers, operating on a global scale. The Ethnos!

If anybody'd know about a damaru, *it'd be an ethnomusicologist.*

Andy was one of the first to join our late-night feeding sessions at the computer; he was the fastest typist I had ever seen. He was also a drummer, which made him a triple threat: computer literate, an ethnomusicologist, and a drummer!

Whenever the opportunity arose, I pressed Andy to tell me stories about the Ethnos. He obliged by explaining that ethnomusicology was an offspring of anthropology and musicology and that neither parent had been particularly pleased by the birth. It had all started with the explosion of interest in anthropology in the late nineteenth century, combined with the fact that Edison's early cylinder recorder was one of the tools of cultural preservation that the early Anthros had taken with them into the field. By the turn of the century archives of "primitive" music had been established in most of the intellectual capitals of the West — Paris, Vienna, Berlin. But these archives were rarely visited by anyone other than the anthropologically inclined, who treated their musical holdings as just more artifacts, gathered because they were collectible, like baskets or war canoes.

Few people thought of these recordings in terms of their musical value; indeed most scholars of music — musicologists — considered them valueless or irrelevant, if they even knew they existed. The only valuable and legitimate music, as far as they were concerned, was Western art music, Bach, Beethoven, Mozart. Anything that smacked of "folk" or "savage" music was anthropology, not musicology.

The first break in this attitude came when a few renegade scholars, like the Germans Curt Sachs, Erich von Hornbostel, and Carl Stumpf, made the obvious argument that it was impossible to understand the evolution of music as an art, to say nothing about the origins of the instruments in the orchestra, without coming to terms with the astonishing information contained in the ethnographies of the anthropologists.

Thanks to these pioneers, along with the American musicologist Charles Seeger, a mutation appeared in the world of scholarship known as "comparative musicology," a subbranch of what was already a subbranch of music. Comparative musicology existed in a minor way until 1950, the year the Dutch musicologist Jaap Kunst published a book entitled *Musicologica: A Study of the Nature of Ethno-musicology, Its Problems, Methods and Representative Personalities*. That one word — *ethno-musicology* — apparently resonated so strongly within the hearts of comparative musicologists everywhere that it was eventually adopted as the tribal name. Subsequent editions of Kunst's book were simply called *Ethnomusicology*, without the hyphen. Five years later the Society for Ethnomusicology was founded.

When Andy and I first talked about the Ethnos, I had an image of them as this shadowy band of hunters and gatherers who were involved in their own Great Hunt, wandering the globe, emerging from the rain forests and the deserts once a year to perform their group rituals in isolated convention halls. They fascinated me. One day I asked Schloss: "So, Andy, if I wanted to talk to the chiefs of your tribe, how would I go about it, where would I find them, who are they?"

Andy suggested I contact a former professor of his, now teaching at the University of California, Santa Cruz, who had been an editor of the tribal journal, *Ethnomusicology*. I didn't talk to this man, Betsy did, but she returned with a list of names and telephone numbers and addresses of places like the Smithsonian and the American Museum of Natural History. In a few weeks the Grateful Dead was embarking upon one of our periodic tours of the East Coast. It seemed the perfect excuse to go and seek out these wise men at their seasonal encampments.

FRITZ KUTTNER TURNED OUT TO BE A SCHOLARLY OLD GENTLEMAN
of close to eighty. He had just come out of the hospital the day before our visit,
but he was still eager to talk. A few minutes after our arrival at his apartment on
New York's Upper West Side, his wife guided him into the library, made him
comfortable on a couch, then went and brought us tea.

"So," he said, as Betsy and I sat there cradling our cups in our laps,
"What do you know about gongs?"

Betsy immediately began telling him of the grant she had gotten to go
to China to study the acoustical properties of gongs, and as I listened I remembered my own gong story:

THE GONG TALE

The Grateful Dead was in Boston on one of our early tours, playing
at a bowling alley that had been turned into a nightclub, and I'd
taken the opportunity to visit the Zildjian factory, which was just
outside the city. The Zildjians were the best cymbal makers in the
world. They had been in the business for at least five hundred years,
the family fortune erected upon a secret formula for how to mix the
molten sounding metals from which fine metallophones are almost
alchemically made. Supposedly some scientists from MIT had tried to
crack the formula using scientific techniques but had failed.

I'd always been attracted to occult stuff like this, so when the Grateful
Dead's schedule brought me to Boston, Ram Rod and I made an
appointment and drove out to the Zildjian factory to examine their
stock of cymbals. The cymbals were kept in a huge vault, rack after
rack of them. I remember them shutting the big steel doors to the
outside factory and we settled in for an afternoon of serious play in
this garden of metal. I took a deep breath and gazed around and saw,
hanging high up near the ceiling, some extraordinary metal disks.
"What are those?" I asked. "Gongs," was the reply. At one time the
Zildjians had thought of importing a line of Chinese gongs and they
had even manufactured a few of their own, but nothing had come of
it; they had been hanging up there for years. A ladder was found and
a workman carefully lowered one of the enormous disks; it was at

THE
early Ethnos.
Clockwise, from top:
Percival R. Kirby
(with flute), Curt
Sachs, Carl Stumpf,
André Schaeffner
(bottom right), Helen
H. Roberts, Ernst
Emsheimer, Jaap
Kunst, A. J. Ellis,
Claudie Marcel-
Dubois, and Erich von
Hornbostel (center).

least five feet in diameter. They lashed it with ropes and tied it to the superstructure that was holding the cymbals. Someone handed me a mallet. Striking the gong was like shooting an arrow of sound into the air with a powerful bow.

The Zildjians gave me every gong in the place. The family patriarch, Avedis Zildjian, had been so pleased that someone had finally appreciated his gongs that he insisted I take them all and play them; it had broken his heart to have them sit there, ignored, for so long.

I played them on stage during that tour and when I got back to the Barn I discovered I couldn't stop playing them. They sent me into a deep trance state full of vivid hallucinations. I asked my psychologist friend, Stanley Krippner, to come listen to these gongs. Krippner later conducted some tests on how quickly and deeply one could induce the hypnotic state with a gong. At the time he determined they were the quickest inducer he knew of.

Fritz Kuttner reportedly had the key to gongs. A scholar of Chinese music, he had been gathering data for fifty years (and in 1990 published a book) to support his thesis that the gong makers of ancient China had possessed techniques of metallophone production far superior to anything in the West, even with today's technology. The picture he painted for us that afternoon was a scenario in which gong-making secrets had been passed down within the metallophone guilds for over 2,000 years, from family to family, generation to generation, until somehow these secrets had been lost. Now only the gongs themselves existed, usually in private collections though occasionally one surfaced. Many years ago a wealthy collector had brought one to the Metropolitan Museum of Art, a magnificent tam-tam gong, where it had been tested by one of the staff technicians, who made the following report of its unique powers:

> One single gentle tap of pianissimo strength with a soft padded drumstick to the cymbal's rim produces the following sound phenomena. A soft hum issues and remains unchanged for about ten seconds; then a gradual crescendo develops over the next 20 seconds and begins to gain enormously in volume after 30 to 35 seconds. After about 60 seconds, a colossal triple fortissimo is reached, which is truly terrifying and close to unbearable; bystanders witnessing the sounding in the large entrance hall of the museum covered their ears and felt like running away from the tremendous roar.

Kuttner had met the technician long after the gong had passed back to the rightful owner, whose name the technician could no longer remember. He had asked the Metropolitan to search its records, but the curators had replied that the records were in such bad shape that it wouldn't be worth their time, or his, to look. And when he'd pressed the matter, they had treated him like a nuisance, not a scholar.

The technician later remembered one additional detail: the owner had been a woman who ran her own dance troupe, and the gong had been her signature stage prop. That was as far as Kuttner had pursued the story. Not that he didn't burn to hear that gong, but at his age, with all the important work he had left to do and now illness, he didn't have time to be Sherlock Holmes. But it was out there, in a basement, hanging on a wall, maybe still being used in a dance troupe.

ON ONE WALL OF TOM VENNUM'S OFFICE WAS A BIG MAP OF THE world with lots of pushpins stuck into it. It was like something out of a James Bond movie:

That red one in the South Pacific, that's Sonneborn, good man on the bullroarer. And that blue one by your cheek, that's . . .

Tom Vennum was the senior ethnomusicologist at the Office of American Folklife Programs at the Smithsonian; his office was Ethno Central as far as the United States went. I'd known we were going to get along as soon as we'd stepped into his Washington rowhouse the night before. The place was filled with drums and art and masks and strange furniture, like the stools Vennum sat us on as he began to tell stories about his expeditions to Haiti to study vôdun (voodoo). Each anecdote came with its own soundtrack. Vennum had hundreds of cassettes and the whole time he was talking to us he was jumping back and forth between the cassette player and his chair. He'd slap on a cassette, rapidly scan to the section he wanted, then pop back to his own stool and continue his story:

Where was I? Oh yes, I did hear a great story about a zombie . . .

For the past couple of years Vennum had been observing and working with one of the last of the traditional Ojibwa drum makers in northern

Wisconsin. As we were leaving, he presented us with copies of the monograph he'd just written about this man, *The Ojibwa Dance Drum*. He also invited us to his office the next day, promising a tour of the catacombs – the Smithsonian is like an iceberg, nine-tenths of it never seen by the public. There are huge storage areas that span out under the National Mall in Washington, room after room of tall metal storage cases full of artifacts such as Maori war canoes, Kwakiutl masks, and lots of skeletons.

The smell of this place was intense, at least for me. It wasn't so much the smell of death, dust, and age, but more a psychological stench of spirits violated. I hated seeing the drums just rotting there, unplayed, their voices going slowly dead, and with them a legacy of rhythm beyond price. I thought of Fritz Kuttner's elusive gong. How many tam-tams were lying in chilly basement rooms like these, waiting for someone to rediscover their mysterious powers?

Perhaps this explained Vennum's enthusiasm for my drum quest. As I sat there looking at the wall map with its forest of colored pins, Vennum was on the phone, lining up museums and archives in cities where the Grateful Dead was scheduled to play. He found me willing researchers, usually Ph.D.s or postdocs, who guided me through the museums and the libraries. I was particularly interested in pictures, and many afternoons were spent poring over thousands of negatives in badly heated museum warehouses.

Dance partners. A lot of them were so energized by their brief time on the hunt that periodically they'd crash the archives and continue the chase on their own. Every few months another little package of data would arrive from them. It was the call of the drum; others were hearing it as well as I.

"WHO'S THIS GUY HERE?"

Vennum followed my finger into the South Pacific, where a yellow pushpin sat in the middle of Papua New Guinea.

"Oh, that's Steve Feld. Brilliant young scholar. The Kaluli. Looks like Dustin Hoffman."

When he wasn't at his address in the rain forest of central Papua New Guinea, Steven Feld was on the faculty of the Annenberg School of Communications at the University of Pennsylvania in Philadelphia. I walked to his

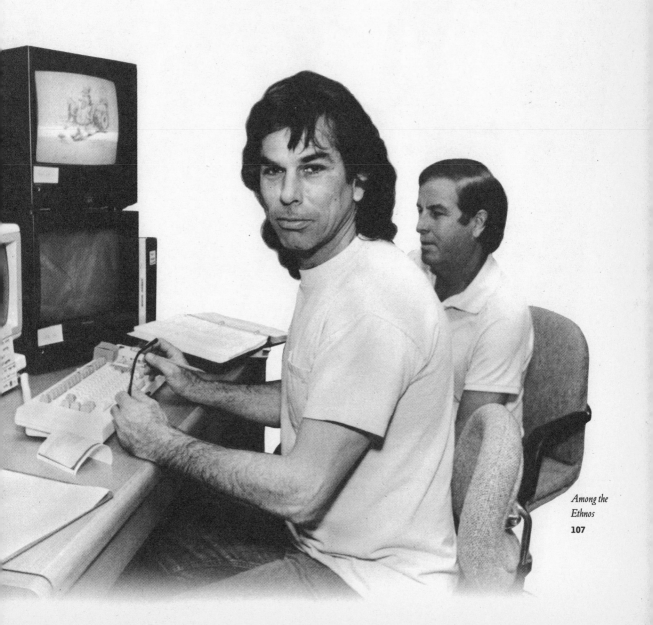

STEVEN FELD
*(right) and a
Kaluli man*

house the morning after a show. His place was classic Ethno; immediately inside the door was an enormous rattan pig mask. Looking at it, and at Feld, who really did look like Dustin Hoffman, I realized how unusual this guy's life was compared to mine and how much I envied his contact with the alien. Feld was one of the first field Ethnos I'd met. For six months of the year he was truly on the Edge. The last time he'd been in Papua New Guinea, he'd spent his time sitting with a parabolic microphone in a tree, recording the complete circadian cycle of the Papua New Guinea jungle – twenty-four hours of rain forest soundscape – which he then condensed down to forty-three minutes. The Voices of the Forest.

Feld also told me a wonderful story of how the tribe he lived with, the Kaluli, made their drums:

The Young Ethno's Tale

The Kaluli – there are only about twelve hundred of them – live just north of the slopes of Mount Bosavi on the Great Papuan Plateau in the Southern Highlands of Papua, Papua New Guinea. They live in what are known as longhouse communities separated from one another by an hour's walk along forest trails. About fifteen families, or roughly sixty people, live in each community.

Technically the Kaluli are horticulturists. Their staple food is *sago,* a root vegetable, though they also maintain large gardens and hunt small animals, wild pigs, and birds.

Their music is primarily vocal and the principal accompaniment is provided by rattles made from mussel shells, crayfish claws and seed pods. But the Kaluli do have a drum, a single-headed conical drum about three feet in length. They call this drum *ilib,* which is also their word for "treehole" and "chest," meaning the upper part of the body. All drum parts are named after human body parts. To produce sound a drum must resound from its head, resonate in the inner chest, and speak from its voice through a mouth.

The Kaluli drum makes a distinctive throbbing sound. The rhythm is regular, about 135 pulses per minute, and at 80 decibels it is one of the loudest sounds a Kaluli can make or hear.

The Kaluli don't live in the same linear way as we do, but if you average it out it takes them about six days to make one of these drums. The first thing they do is cut down a kind of magnolia tree known as a *dona;* other wood is sometimes used, but the *dona* is preferred because of its lightness and resonant qualities. Once the tree is toppled, a four-foot section is cut off and soaked in water, to prepare it for hollowing.

On the second day the log is removed from the water. With a combination of burning, scraping with bamboo, and sanding with rough leaves, one end is hollowed out for about two feet. Then the other end is hollowed until there is just a tiny bridge of wood remaining between the two hollowed-out sections, about two inches thick. Again the log is returned to the water to soak.

On the third day no work is done on the drum. Instead a hunting party is convened to capture a *tibodai* bird, whose whistlelike voice is thought to be the spirit of a dead child. This can take several days. Once the bird has been caught, its feathers are plucked and placed inside the drum. Then, in the most dramatic aspect of the process, the throat and tongue of the *tibodai* are placed on the wooden bridge that separates the two hollowed out sections. The bridge is then cut out, while the drum maker recites a magical saying, which I'm not permitted to reveal.

The head of the drum is generally made from the skin of a *yobo* lizard, although the skin of snakes and other lizards is sometimes used. The skin is fixed to the rim of the drum using a gluey latex made from tree bark and tied down with cane, then dried in the sun or over a low fire.

After the head has dried, four lumps of beeswax are placed on it and again a magical saying is softly recited, ensuring that these lumps will now throb like the heart of a bush dog.

Drumming is usually performed for four or five hours as a late-afternoon prelude to an all-night major ceremony. One to five drummers, wearing elaborate feather costumes and dancing while they drum, are placed at either end of the longhouse. As the pulses blend together, a transformation occurs in the drum voice. Instead of the throbbing *tibo-tibo-tibo* of the *tibodai* bird, the Kaluli say the drums begin to cry *dowo-dowo-dowo,* the word for "father." These, say the Kaluli, are the spirits of dead children calling out to their fathers. Hearing this, everyone begins to weep.

"DO YOU KNOW THE OLD CHINESE STORY," THE PROFESSOR ASKED ME when we first met, "about the disciple who went to study music – the zither actually – with a famous master who was a hermit? Every day the master would play and the student would just listen. One day the teacher said, 'Why don't you try so I can hear what you're learning?' And the student said, 'Until I have the spirit of the music in my heart, there's no sense in playing it on the strings.' This went on for several years. Then one day the student sat down and played and it was clear he'd become a master himself. That's one of the better parables I know about the importance of spirit and the unimportance of technique."

This was Schloss's mentor, Fredric Lieberman. Short, balding, wearing thick glasses, and living in a house that was like a library with a bed in it, the professor was an archetype come to life. That was my first impression, in any case. The man was a virtual walking encyclopedia of Ethno lore. He not only knew almost everybody in the field of ethnomusicology, but he also knew what they had written, what their teachers had written, and what their teachers' teachers had written. And when. Whatever topic I raised, he could reel off eight or ten articles, a couple of books, or the telephone number of just the right scholar to call.

As I got to know the professor better, I had to revise my original image of him as a typical mild-mannered academic. When it came to gathering information, he was a cold-blooded hunter. What Fred really liked was the challenge of the chase, and he had often regretted that you couldn't make a living in this culture as a sort of private eye of learning, a Sam Spade of the information age, sitting in your nondescript office, a fifth of bourbon on your desk alongside your Magnum .357 and your modem, waiting for a grieving blonde widow to walk through the door and ask you about the connection between the sistrum and the Isis cult.

I might not have been the grieving blonde he expected, but the notion of chasing the drum captivated him. He knew immediately that it was an important story, one that had to be told. We made our first run together at the Berkeley library. The professor had spent his life working the stacks; he was like a streetwise cop as he glided through the opening-day-of-semester crush. The library, I realized, was his turf.

The way Fred handled the books he wanted to look at really impressed and taught me something. He treated them very gently. He didn't bang them on the table or carelessly turn the pages. There was a tenderness to the way he held them.

Temperamentally, we were the tortoise and the hare. I remember, about the fourth Saturday, sitting there looking at the stack of books with Fred bent fondly over them, and thinking that I was going about this all wrong. The professor was an idea man, not a leg man. I decided to hire him some assistants to do the finding and just let him concentrate on his talent for pursuit of the subject.

We assembled a research team and began meeting every week. Assignments were given ("Let's collect all the names for bullroarers around the world") and the previous week's information collected, to be sent down to Stanford and entered on the mainframe. At Karma I used to sit at a terminal and make endless lists:

> *Supernatural powers of drums*
> *Consecration of drums*
> *Primeval slime? Primordial slime?*
> *Instruments associated with cosmologies*
> *Use of drum as catalyst in metamorphosis*
> *Extinct instruments; myths telling stories of creation of instruments*
> *Traveling dentists — drum use by European dentists in Middle Ages —*
>   *need more information on this!!*
> *Intricacies governing the pulse*
> *Percussion and transition*

"Percussion and transition." During our first conversation I had told Fred about my belief that drums were intimately connected with altered states of consciousness. He'd said, "Percussion and Transition." This, it turned out, was the name of a little debate that had been going on in social sciences since the late sixties when the eminent British anthropologist Rodney Needham had published a small essay with that title in the journal *Man*, calling attention to the fact that percussion was almost universally used during such rituals of transition as birth, puberty, marriage, and death, when the spirit world is called upon for guidance.

On the book cover:

45 SIÈCLES DE
MUSIQUE
DANS
L'ÉGYPTE ANCIENNE
À TRAVERS LA SCULPTURE, LA PEINTURE, L'INSTRUMENT

HANS HICKMANN

Needham asked, "Why is noise that is produced by striking or shaking so widely used in order to communicate with the other world?" Fred and I picked up Needham on one of our feeding runs in the library. What fascinated me was the picture that emerged of the way information was shared among intellectuals. Needham hadn't pretended to know the answer; he was just posing a question. The next issue of *Man* included several reasoned responses to Needham. A couple directed his attention to an article published a few years earlier in the field of acoustics, "A Physiological Explanation of Unusual Behavior in Ceremonies Involving Drums," authored by a psychologist named Andrew Neher. Studying drumming in a laboratory setting, Neher found that he was able to "drive" or "entrain" the brainwaves of his experimental subjects down into what is called the alpha/theta border, which means that a majority of the electrical activity in their brains was pulsing at a rate of between six and eight cycles per second.

During activity the brain predominantly pulses in alpha and beta, or between twelve to thirty cycles per second. Theta is the zone of electrical activity the brain decelerates into right before sleep, or the delta state, when we pulse at between two to four cycles per second, with a little spike of activity every ninety minutes or so that accompanies dreaming. Theta is that period of drifting right before sleep when all sorts of thoughts and memories wash through consciousness, and we are as liable to remember where we lost our hat as suddenly unravel the mystery of death.

Neher theorized that percussion, particularly drumming, fulfilled the role of "driver" because drums produced a sound that was so dense, so inharmonic, so fast-decaying and scattered across the frequency band that it overloaded the hearing mechanism. And it was this overloading that helped induce trance.

For a couple of months Neher was my man. I thought he'd given me the answer to my question about drums and trance — auditory driving, the fact that percussive sound was ideally suited to overload the basilar membrane of the ear. But critiques of Neher gradually came my way, poking holes in his experimental design. Gilbert Rouget in *Music and Trance* sneered that "if Neher were right, half of Africa would be in a trance from the beginning of the year to the end." According to Rouget, trance was trance and music was music, and there was no way to prove that one could induce the other; the best you could say was that sometimes music accompanied the trance state, but just as often it didn't.

I later called up Neher, who lived near Santa Cruz, and one afternoon Fred and I paid him a visit. Neher hadn't given his paper on drumming and auditory driving five minute's thought in twenty-five years, so he was more than a little startled to find himself at the center of a debate that was taking place totally unbeknownst to him. We showed him Rouget's critique and a few months later he sent us a copy of a letter that he was mailing to Rouget, refuting him point by point. In his cover letter, Neher stressed that the question of whether percussive sound could drive brainwaves was still an unanswered one, for the simple reason that no one had yet done the experiments.

Another of the responses to Needham's article came from John Blacking, of Queens University, Belfast. Its tone was lofty and dismissive – "I would not question the assumption that there is a connexion between transition and noise organized rhythmically by human beings, because this aspect of the hypothesis contains the germ of a truth known to musicians throughout the world" – but what attracted my attention to this letter in particular was the fact that Blacking was the only one who mentioned the possibility that the musician might be able to shed some light on this problem.

The real knowing is in the playing.

Shortly after first noticing his name, I learned that this same John Blacking was coming to Berkeley to deliver an address, which Fred and I decided to attend. Blacking turned out to be a tall, lean, distinguished scholar whose accent was too thick for my brain to handle; I literally did not understand a word he said. I heard him okay, but in terms of comprehension I was living in a mud hut in the valley while John Blacking was halfway up the mountain, talking to the gods.

Fred understood it. He knew Blacking, having run into him at various Ethno councils. Blacking had a theory, Fred told me, that the key to our rapid evolution lay in our mastery of external rhythms, starting with the simplest flint tools and progressing through dance, language, and music. A few days after the lecture, Fred arranged for us to meet Professor Blacking. He greeted us cordially and listened politely as we explained our drum project. We painted a bright big picture for him, ran down the whole list of things we were interested in, none of which seemed to spark much enthusiasm. When we mentioned we were also searching for myths about the origins of drums, he said, "Forget about myths, don't waste your time; that's the past. Find out what the drum does to the body.

"Find out about rhythm."

WE ARE
*composed of rhythms
and surrounded by
rhythms.*

CHAPTER EIGHT

The Big Clock

ERE IS THE MYSTERY:
If the rhythm is right, if the translation between inner mood and drum membrane is perfect, then you know it instantly. *Ahhhh,* you say, this goes with my body tempo, this relates to how I feel today, how fast my heart is beating, what my thoughts are, what my hands feel like.

When the rhythm is right you feel it with all your senses; it's in your mind, in your body, in both places. The head of the drum vibrates as the stick strikes it. The physical feedback is almost instantaneous, rushing along your arms, filling your ears. A feeling not unlike trust settles over you as you give yourself to the rhythm. You don't fight it, but instead allow yourself to be

117

propelled by this insistent but friendly feeling. All sense of the present moment disappears, the normal categories of time become meaningless.

Your mind is turned off, your judgment wholly emotional. Your emotions seem to stream down your arms and legs and out the mouth of the drum; you feel light, gravityless, your arms feel like feathers. You fly like a bird. When the rhythm is right.

Here is the mystery and I don't think it can be solved, certainly not with words or numbers.

"Find out what rhythm is doing to the body," Blacking had said, and it was like a fog lifting. *Rhythm's the key, not drumming, not noise. The man's right. Find out about rhythm!* And I tried. I assembled the documents; I gathered the data; I spoke to as many learned men and women as I could find. I discovered that rhythm is a paradoxical, difficult thing to think about; as soon as you begin pursuing the mystery of rhythm, you are forced to confront the even deeper mystery of time.

You can't talk about rhythm without talking about time. Rhythm is what time *does,* whether it comes to us in the pattern of the seasons or in the pattern on the face of a Rolex watch. Or better still, it's what we do with time. We chop up time, impose patterns on it, tease regularities out of it, and then confuse them with time itself, although the regularities observed by a New Yorker will be vastly different from those of a Trobriand Islander.

Rhythm and time — as a drummer I make my living keeping time in a musical ensemble, and the way I do this is by turning noise into rhythm using percussion.

"THE ORDER IN THE MOVEMENT" — THAT'S HOW PLATO DEFINED rhythm. Of time, he said it is the "moving image of eternity."

I had little quotes like this stuck all over the Timeline. Proverbs. Profundities. A lot of them I didn't understand. Like this one from the biologist and writer Lewis Thomas: "Music is the effort we make to explain to ourselves how the mind works. . . . If you want, as an experiment, to hear the whole mind working, all at once, put on *St. Matthew Passion* and turn the volume all the way up. That is the sound of the whole central nervous system of human beings, all at once."

Or this, from Professor Blacking himself: "Music is given to us with the sole purpose of establishing an order in things, including *the coordination between man and time.*" Or, from the Greek mystic and mathematician Pythagoras: "A stone is frozen music."

A few years ago a German jazz historian named Joachim Ernst-Berendt published a book called *Nada Brahma: The World Is Sound,* in which he proposed that (*a*) since the one sure thing we can say about fundamental matter is that it is vibrating and (*b*) since all vibrations are theoretically sound, then (*c*) it is not unreasonable to suggest that the universe is music and should be perceived as such. In which case perceiving a stone as frozen music would be perfectly appropriate. I like Berendt's metaphor too much to quibble over the details, but I would add that since vibrations are also rhythms, then everything is rhythm too. The universe is also rhythm.

We're too slow to register the microrhythms of our universe – the dance of atoms and molecules – in any conscious way, just as we're too fast to recognize some of the macrorhythms that we're involved in. The longer the rhythm the harder it is to study. Astronomers would love to chart our solar system's dance through the Milky Way, except it takes us 240 million years to complete one cycle.

One of the first laws of rhythm is repetition – a cycle is something that recurs or repeats. There is no rhythm without repetition. Once you've observed enough repetitions you can say there's a pattern, and patterns are something we're taught to scan for. *Strike a membrane with a stick, the ear fills with noise – unmelodious, inharmonic sound. Strike it a second time, a third, you've got rhythm.*

What has science given us in the last century but an increasingly rich knowledge of the rhythms that rule our time on this planet? Rhythm piled atop rhythm, with even the simplest one-celled creature vibrating on distinct atomic, molecular, subcellular, and cellular levels. To say nothing of the on/off rhythm of neurons firing in the brain, the butterfly rhythms of the heart, the mysterious rhythm that brings the swallows back to Capistrano. We are embedded in a universe of rhythms, which means we are embedded in a universe of time.

We live on a planet that completes its cycle around the sun every three hundred and sixty-five days, with a moon that cycles around us every twenty-eight days, and we rotate around our own axis every twenty-four hours. Most of us have little appreciation, however, for just how deeply we are dancing to these

rhythms. There is a direct connection between these cosmic cycles and our bodily ones, most profoundly with respect to the circadian dance of day and night. This cycle of light and darkness is fundamental to all biological functioning on this planet. All organic life divides its circadian time into periods of activity and rest. Dogs and humans, for example, are active during the day and quiet at night. Cats and owls are just the opposite. But the activity/rest continuum is only the most obvious example. Body temperature, blood pressure, respiration, pulse, blood sugar, hemoglobin levels, amino acid levels, appetite — all are influenced by the planet's daily revolution.

Within the body itself the main rhythm is laid down by the cardiovascular system, the heart and the lungs, the heart beating between sixty to eighty times per minute, the lungs filling and emptying at about a quarter that speed. But again these are only the most obvious bodily rhythms. From the vibration of single cells to the slow peristalsis of our intestines, our internal machinery is all moving in a complex dance whose synchronization is carefully monitored by the central nervous system, which then reports on the state of our internal rhythms to the midbrain. Unless we have been exercising hard or are menstruating or are sick, we are rarely conscious of our internal rhythms and almost never conscious of the way our bodies reflect the larger rhythms of the planet, solar system, universe.

Science knows one big thing about rhythm, something it calls the Law of Entrainment. The Law of Entrainment, which seems to be fundamental to the universe, was first discovered in 1665 by the Dutch scientist Christian Huygens. Huygens noticed that if two clocks were placed next to each other, within a very short time they would lock up and tick in perfect synchrony. *Entrainment.* If two rhythms are nearly the same, and their sources are in close proximity, they will always entrain. Why? The best theory is that nature is efficient and it takes less energy to pulse together than in opposition.

One way to think about the connection between those universal and planetary rhythms and the personal rhythms of our own bodies is that we are entrained with these larger patterns, we are pulsing in synch with them because nature is efficient and we are a part of nature.

BECAUSE
we dance through time in a group, we have to learn how to synchronize our personal rhythms with those of our fellow creatures.

HERE IS ANOTHER MYSTERY. WE ARE COMPOSED OF RHYTHMS AND SUR-rounded by rhythms, yet we come out of the womb incapable of performing even the most rudimentary of rhythms, like opening and closing our hands. A baby horse within minutes of birth is up and cantering around. It takes us months to figure out how to move our legs in proper hominid fashion, with one limb supporting the body as the other swings forward, plants itself, and pre-pares to support the body as the other swings forward, and so on.

Our first rhythmic body movement is an instinctual sucking move-ment we make with our mouths, which is followed, at the age of about two and a half months, by the ability to beat our feet in a controlled manner. At six months we can sit up and rock our body from side to side, backward and for-ward, up and down. At about eight months we're scooting along on our hands and knees and still rocking. By a year we're taking our first steps.

Although sensitivity to external rhythms shows up at about the age of two months, we can't consciously maintain a beat, in the sense of following a rhythm produced by a metronome or a clock, until about our fourth year. The key to duplicating a rhythm apparently lies in our ability to measure the spaces between the beats. In music we call this keeping time. Just about everybody can synchronize with a rhythm if the time between beats is 400 to 800 milliseconds. But if you ask people to handle a beat that is faster or slower, the percentage of those who can drops off fast. And it practically disappears if you ask people to tap after the beat.

Average those two figures together and you come up with an ideal time of 600 milliseconds, or a bit longer than one beat every half second. That same figure – one beat every 600 milliseconds – corresponds with the tempo of an average heartbeat and the tempo of our walking, as well as with the most rapid tempo of those early sucking movements. It's as close to an ideal human rhythm as scientists have been able to discover.

Because we dance through time in a group, we have to learn how to synchronize our personal rhythms with those of our fellow creatures. We do this by creating group clocks that allow us to keep time together. To be effec-tive, these group clocks must take into consideration both the natural and bio-logical rhythms.

Hunters and gatherers construct their clocks from the natural cycles of the plants and animals that form their diet. Agricultural communities con-struct their clocks out of the cycle of planting, germination, and harvest. The principal clock of the Andaman Islanders, for example, is tied to the flowering cycle in their part of the jungle; they know where they are in time because of how the jungle smells. The San of South Africa use a banana as a clock. When the hunters embark on a long trip they take an unripe banana with them. When the banana has ripened, they know it's time to start for home. We, on the other hand, are descended from cultures that found their clocks in the rhythm of the stars, although for the last four hundred years we have embraced an increasingly linear concept of time.

Our word *religion* comes from the Latin and means "to bind together." A working religion, then, might be one that binds together the many rhythms that affect us by creating techniques – rituals – that attempt to synchronize the three dances, the personal, the cultural, and the cosmic. If the technique works, the reward is a new dimension of rhythm and time – the sacred.

I REMEMBER SITTING WITH FRED IN JOHN BLACKING'S OFFICE AT BERKELEY, thinking that here was a man who at least knew what the question was, though whether he had the answer I couldn't say, since most of his conversation was in that peculiar code that academics use among themselves.

Blacking thought that the ability to perceive rhythm was one of the fundamental properties of the human brain. He suspected there was a strong connection between our rapid evolution and our ability to recognize, externalize, and control rhythms – the vocal rhythms that would become language, the bodily rhythms that would give us our first advanced technology, and the larger natural rhythms, like the lunar cycle, which we began recording on little stone batons. The tool record, for Blacking – all those chipped arrowheads and scrapers – was basically just a marvelous material illustration of our dramatic encounter with rhythm.

As was music. With the rhythmic clacking of the concussion sticks and the cry of the human voice we began exploring the delightful discovery that we could impose patterns not just on the rocks we made into tools or on the mimicking body that danced our dances, but also on this unseen and mysterious world of sound. And we could generate this world of sound not just with our own body, but with literally everything that surrounded us.

Dig a hole in the ground, place a board over it, stamp on it — you've made a stamping pit. Take two clamshells, clap them between your palms. Pick up the jawbone of a bison, rasp it with a femur.

But Blacking believed that music was a special case. It wasn't just another example of our ability to master rhythm; it was the mystery of rhythm itself in a microcosm. According to Blacking, music was a mirror that reflected a culture's deepest social and biological rhythms; it was an externalization of the pulses that remained hidden beneath the busyness of daily life. In the making of music you saw the mystery at work.

To make music, a musician has to learn how to control his or her biological rhythms — the heartbeat, the breath — focusing the body on producing, either vocally or with an instrument, the specific vibrations that flow out into the world of sound. But that's only the first step. To make music as a group, each musician has to learn how to entrain to the larger rhythm.

If the rhythm is right, you feel it with all your senses; it's in your mind, your body, in both places.

Get a group of musicians vibrating harmoniously together and you have one of the most powerful emotional experiences on the planet, one that would be impossible if we hadn't evolved the conscious ability to entrain ourselves rhythmically.

A large part of music's power and pleasure, says Blacking, comes from its ability to reconnect the player and the listener with the deeper rhythms they're unconscious of. It accomplishes this by taking us out of the clock-ticking world of ordinary time and into a special world of time that Blacking called virtual time.

FOR ME THE MYSTERY BEGAN WITH THE RUDIMENTS. THAT STEADY measured right-right-left-right-left-right-left-left was my first introduction to rhythm. It was very visual. Each rudiment was like a game of tic-tac-toe that, once played, became an interlocking piece in a larger rhythmic puzzle. A good rudimental drummer was someone who could play both games at the same time, fluently weaving the little pattern into the bigger one.

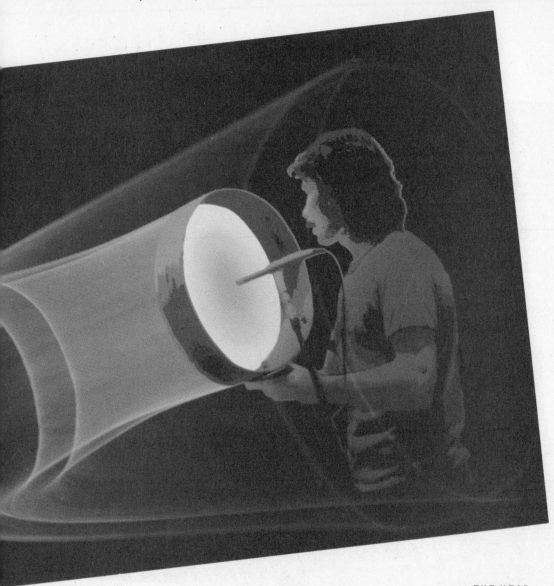

THE HEAD
*of the drum vibrates as
the stick strikes it. The
physical feedback is
almost instantaneous,
rushing along your
arms, filling your ears.*

*The Big
Clock*

125

Next came Krupa. My mother often played Gene Krupa, the Carnegie Hall performances, Big Band music with a solid drum backbeat. She also had a number of Folkways albums, early ethnomusicological recordings, I now realize, of things like Caribbean drumming and Mississippi blues, which I used to play much more than she did. From these I learned that there were many different kinds of rhythms, that each distinctive music developed an equally distinctive rhythm to drive it through time.

When I was in my early teens I watched the Latin rhythms from Cuba invade New York and sweep aside all the other rhythms. Bands like Tito Puente and Machito were giant rhythm machines. They played a style of music that had a thin little line of melody running over a huge rush of rhythm. Played it all night long, without pause, five or six bands smoothly segueing into each other until dawn. There was no applause or even casual listening. These rhythms were so big they lifted you from your chair and dragged you out onto the floor. You *had* to dance.

A few months out of high school I discovered the work of the Nigerian drummer Olatunji, and a few years after that I secured my present job as a drummer in the Grateful Dead, and a few months after that I met a true rhythmist who taught me that rhythm was just time and time could be cut up any way you wanted, though certain dissections were more interesting than others — a lesson I'm still learning.

Everything is rhythm and time. Wind rustling through a tree — there's a rhythm there; give it enough time and you'll hear it. Quiet yourself and eventually you'll start hearing the rhythms of nature. Or feeling them. Quiet yourself and focus inside and eventually you'll start feeling your own biorhythms, what one of my Timeline philosophers called "the silent orchestra."

Everything has time but if you started keeping track of all the different times you'd go crazy. Everything has a clock — the growing of the trees, the flight of birds, the movement of mice in the walls of the house once night falls, the cars outside on the road to the coast. The road outside my house has a powerful rhythm, as do the powerlines that run alongside it. In the last hundred years a web of electrical cables has been spun around the planet — there is almost no place that is not bathed by energy made to pulse at fifty or sixty cycles per second. Does the Law of Entrainment operate at this level? Are we being entrained rhythmically by the electrical environment with which we're surrounded?

For nine months we live in the womb, listening to the orchestra of our mother, entrained with her. Then we are born and the first thing that happens is a massive dose of rhythm. Our lungs begin pumping, our heartbeat settles into its steady pulse, our senses begin scanning; vibrations rush into the eyes and ears, up the nose, into the mouth, pulsing against the newborn skin.

It must be the biggest shock of life, this onslaught of rhythms that want to drag us out onto the floor and make us dance.

There is an old Arab proverb: "He who makes a mistake is still our friend; he who adds to, or shortens, a melody is still our friend; but he who violates a rhythm unawares can never be our friend." Ishaq ibn Ibrahim said that in the ninth century. What he meant was that if you're at least listening, if you're aware that you're violating the rhythm, then you will know enough to stop and figure out where you are. But if you violate the rhythm unawares, you ruin everything because you don't stop, making it difficult or impossible for those who are in time to keep playing.

Here is the mystery, and the best advice I can offer you is to make a rhythm of your own and try to entrain with it. For me the best way to make a rhythm is with noise.

The head of the drum vibrates as the stick strikes it. The physical feedback is almost instantaneous, rushing along your arms, filling your ears.

Rhythm and noise.

CHAPTER NINE

Portrait Of A Drummer At The Edge Of Noise

LL MY LIFE NOISE has attracted me. If there was a parade when I was a kid, I'd always be as close to the drums as I could get, running alongside for block after block. The hairs on the back of my neck quivered with excitement as the snare drums, in perfect synch, roared out their rhythmic tattoos. The bass drum was like a blow to the stomach, leaving me breathless. Those were special moments, yet in many respects noise was what an Ethno might call my natal soundscape. I was imprinted by the industrial urban world of my Brooklyn boyhood just as powerfully as the Kaluli are imprinted by the jungle soundscape of Papua New Guinea.

129

Twenty feet from Grandfather's house a trolley kept up an insistent, clattering rhythm. It was the timekeeper, pulsing every twenty to forty minutes, never diminishing or increasing, rain or shine, summer or winter, dawn or dusk. At the other extreme, humming and atonally melodic, was the constant surge of traffic up and down Nostrand Avenue, flowing into the big artery of Quentin Road. And layered in on top was the drone of TVs and radios, exuberant sometimes angry yelling, and the slap-slap-slap of gangs of kids running the territory. Loud, percussive, industrial, urban sound.

I've always been temperamentally on the side of untamed sound. If it was charged with the unexpected, then I loved it. It didn't have to be aggressive; it could be soft like a raindrop or sharp and harsh like a barking dog. The point is, it tugged at me with an almost painful excitement.

I had a whole file in the Anaconda, my computer information tree, devoted to noise quotes.

From the movie *The Buddy Holly Story:*

Mrs. Holly: "What's all that noise?"
Buddy: "Oh, that's just rock and roll."

From bandmate Jerry Garcia:

I come from a folk purist background, so the whole notion of noise is a little alien. But I remember one time when Pigpen and Phil and Weir and I went up to Los Trancos, in the hills up above Palo Alto. It was back when we were the Warlocks, playing divorcée's bars down the Peninsula. So, we're up there on this hilltop, and this jet coming in for a landing comes right over our heads, and the sound that it made just absolutely split the universe — the vortex from its engines — and we're standing there and it was like somebody comes through and just wipes the slate clean! I mean that noise just took everything, it took all of history with it. The sound was absolutely cataclysmic, a huge sound. Right there for me was a moment in which everything — all sound, music, and everything else included — was born again. That was the moment when noise became a useful part of my musical vocabulary. I started working for a long time to get my guitar to sound like a jet plane.

From *The Oxford English Dictionary:*

Noise: (1) Loud outcry, clamour or shouting; din or disturbance made by one or more persons. (2) Common talk, rumor, report; also evil report, slander, scandal. (3) A loud or harsh sound of any kind, a din. (4) A sound which is not remarkably loud. (5) An agreeable or melodious sound — now rare.

My own:

Musicians have to come to grips with their noisiness. Does a painter reject some colors out of hand because they are not beautiful? Should a musician reject some sounds out of hand?

From Andy Schloss:

You can take any sound, and if you make it short enough, it's noise.

From Luigi Russolo, writing in his 1913 futurist manifesto, *The Art of Noises:*

Noise was not really born before the nineteenth century, with the advent of machinery. Today noise reigns supreme over human sensibility. For several centuries, life went on silently, or mutedly. The loudest noises were neither intense, prolonged, nor varied. In fact, nature is normally silent, except for storms, hurricanes, avalanches, cascades, and earthquakes. This is why man was amazed by the first sounds he obtained out of a hole in reeds or a stretched string.

I liked Russolo's philosophy so much I got permission to reprint his manifesto. I still dream about putting it out as a $1.95 paperback, sort of as a corrective to most people's bias about noise.

More Russolo:

Music has developed into a search for a greater variety of instrumental tones and coloring, the most complex succession of dissonant chords, thus preparing the ground for musical noise.

All of us have enjoyed the harmonies of the great masters. Now we are fed up with them. This is why we get infinitely more pleasure imagining combinations of the sounds of trolleys, autos, and loud crowds, than listening once more to the heroic or pastoral symphonies.

Noise accompanies every manifestation of life — it is familiar to us. And noise has the power to bring us back to life. On the other hand, music, an occasional event foreign to life, strikes our ears no more than an overly familiar face does our eye. Noise, gushing confusedly and irregularly out of life, is never totally revealed to us, and keeps in store innumerable surprises. In selecting and coordinating all noises we will enrich mankind with an unsuspected voluptuousness.

All my life noise has attracted me, yet I was twenty-three before I really consummated the attraction. The rudiments — precise, controlled — were at heart the opposite of noise. So were my Big Band, Sonny Payne-type fantasies. I'm almost embarrassed by the tameness of my early dreams of musical success. They are a good lesson in how the imagination is bounded by its environment, a good lesson in how hard it really is to find the Edge, unless you are lucky enough to blunder across a guide, as I did with Billy Kreutzmann, who took me to the Matrix where Janis Joplin and James Gurley and the rest of Big Brother and the Holding Company cracked open my comfortable little notions about music. In my excited and defenseless state I let myself be ravaged.

Kreutzmann and I became drum brothers after that first night at the Matrix. We started hanging out, drumming together, cruising around Haight-Ashbury in Billy's Mustang. The Haight was as noisy as you got in America in the mid-sixties, probably because it was a psychoactive community, maybe the first in the history of the planet. You can't talk about the Haight without taking into account the mutating presence of LSD. People were high all the time. Leonard Wolf, a professor at one of the local colleges and an early Haight watcher, compared it to "an anthill where all the ants are drunk but busy and somehow, when all the tumult has died down, successful." LSD turned up the volume and all those things the conscious mind edits out as useless noise — spiritual epiphanies, paranoid fantasies, imaginative leaps of connection — suddenly came blaring through, loud and clear.

What I remember best about the Haight was the incredible feeling of creativity. Everybody was an artist, whether they had a craft that our culture would recognize as "art" or not. Everybody was high with the spirit of adventurous exploration; everybody was busy becoming new.

Billy invited me to the rehearsals of his band. A couple of times I left the drum store early and tried to connect with them, but I could never seem to find the right warehouse where they were rehearsing. I finally saw them play on September 29, 1967, at a little place called the Straight Theater.

The only thing I'd heard about the band was that its lead singer, a guy named Pigpen, was a Hell's Angel look-alike. I remember that the band was playing a kind of blues, the tempos speeding up and slowing down in unfamiliar yet not awkward places, so the music almost seemed to be breathing, like it was alive. And it was LOUD!

After a two-hour set, Billy and I got together at the break. I was really excited, enthusing about his band's energy and loudness, when he said, "Let's

have some fun. Let's round up some drums and you can sit in for the second set." We dashed outside, got into a truck, and drove over to a friend's house. We grabbed his drums, drove back to the Straight, set up as fast as we could, and launched right into the first song of the next set, a tune they'd been fooling around with called "Alligator/Caution." Everything had been so frantic that it was only then, as the song gathered speed, that I was able to focus on the fact that I didn't have a clue as to what I was supposed to play. Up in front of me was this guy Pigpen, growling out, "Alligator creeping round my doooorrrr."

Next to him was the lead guitarist, Jerry Garcia, who had his amp cranked up, his fingers just soaring up and down the frets, the notes rapidly cascading in a strange way that only became clear much later when Garcia told me he was originally a banjo player and lately he'd been trying to play a kind of banjo-guitar.

Next to Garcia was the bass player, Phil Lesh, who was sort of contracting and expanding his long thin body as he played a bass line that was also expanding and contracting, like a whale coming to the surface then diving, then changing its mind and surfacing again.

Beyond Lesh was Bobby Weir, who was making little running slashing movements as he played rhythm guitar. This sweet, gentle guy – the youngest member of the group – played like a baby-faced killer as he rammed his guitar at his stack of amps.

Next to me was at least a guy I knew, Billy, who was dancing effortlessly at his drums, laying down a natural rock pulse. I remember feeling impressed with how serious they all were – they were really into their instruments – and yet it wasn't an oppressive kind of seriousness. The underlying ethic was to have fun and hope to go someplace musically new.

One of the things Billy had stressed about his band was that the unexpected was welcome, indeed was actively sought – so I threw away my caution and dove in. I remember the feeling of being whipped into a jetstream, but I was so busy drumming that I didn't have time to think about what was happening until "Alligator/Caution" ended some two hours later. It had lasted the whole set. I felt so calm, afterward, so *clean,* as if I'd taken a long steamy shower.

You practice for years so that you reach a point of technical proficiency where the instrument becomes part of your body. You no longer have to think about fingering or counting beats, so your mind is free for higher matters, most of which involve the pursuit of a personal style, a distinctive voice. This is a doubly difficult passage because your training has involved learning to mimic the powerful voices of the great musicians within your tradition, the Krupas, the Riches, the Paynes. You work to become like them, to wear their technical clothing, and yet one day a moment like the one I experienced at the Straight Theater comes along — so totally unexpected that I have often wondered what might have happened if I hadn't crossed paths with Kreutzmann. Would I be running a drum store somewhere, attending rudimental competitions on the weekends, perhaps teaching drum corps like Lenny?

At the end of the set we all embraced, wordlessly. Garcia later told me that everyone had felt it when I finally synched up. Suddenly, with two drums pounding away in the back, they had glimpsed the possibility of a groove so monstrous it would eat the audience. There seemed no question that it was an adventure we would all explore together.

On the bus — just like that.

MUCH HAS BEEN WRITTEN ABOUT MY COLLEAGUES IN THE GRATEFUL Dead, so I'll confine myself to a few first impressions. The main thing, I think, was that we were all noisy guys; we were all in love with noise, each in his own way.

For Pigpen, the vehicle was the blues, and noise was the psychic pain that came out of the African-American experience of slavery and oppression. This son of a rhythm-and-blues disc jockey seemed to have a direct connection with this pain. The blues were Pigpen's truth and he leaned hard on them. Alcohol was his drug and he died of it when he was twenty-seven. Behind his forbidding exterior hid a man who was lovely and gentle.

Phil Lesh was the band's intellectual. He had been to music school. Noise to him was dissonance. He knew about the atonal experimentation of Western art music from Schoenberg and Webern on, and he was applying these orchestral techniques to the traditional rock and roll bass line. Phil created a new instrument out of the bass, fanning the strings with dense, thunderous, sensual chords that could rattle your bones. He could see the musical possibilities in anything.

ON THE BUS –
just like that.
Clockwise, from
bottom: Hart, Garcia,
Kreutzmann, Pigpen,
Weir, Lesh (center).

Bobby Weir's relationship to noise was social. He had grown up in an upper-class enclave in the Bay Area, very proper, very tame. He fled to the loudness and freedom of rock like a refugee going over the wall.

Jerry Garcia had been a folkie, so he didn't think of himself as a noisy guy, but he was. The banjo is a damned loud instrument, if you think about it; it's a rhythmic instrument, the fifth string acting as a droning pulse that everything else plays off of; the banjo even has a membrane, like a drum. Deep down I always suspected Garcia wanted to be a drummer. He was wide open to noise, and when he switched to amplified guitar, he went instantly to the high end of things, and the notes came screaming out of his guitar like those jets he had once wanted to emulate.

Kreutzmann was the exception that proves the rule, so to speak. He wasn't noisy; he had been blessed with an ability to find the beat and lock onto it; he was naturally smooth and in time, which made him irreplaceable. He was the center pole that allowed the rest of us to go roaming off the edges. But it wouldn't have worked if Kreutzmann hadn't been comfortable and energized by the noise we all collectively made.

Everyone wanted to get louder. Every band I knew was in a frenzy for more amplifiers. Groups that formerly could be transported in the back of a VW van now required a bread truck. We were pushing the edge of noise, unwittingly activating our adrenals, and this accounted for the almost breathless thrill that we felt in the presence of this loud music, as though we were riding the roller coaster at Coney Island, not just standing on the stage at the Fillmore. There was a physicality to the music that I hadn't noticed before. After a particularly loud set people couldn't walk or talk right; their speech was slurred. Sometimes head colds vanished.

An immediate problem for Kreutzmann and me was keeping up with the increasingly noisy guitarists. Adding the second drum set was like waving a red flag at their amp lust. We found ourselves in the difficult position of playing acoustic instruments in the middle of an electronic revolution. For a while we just played harder. Every night was like a six-hour marathon combined with fifteen rounds in the ring. Billy and I would be hyperventilating like crazy, while below and in front of us, strolling languidly around, occasionally drifting over to their amps to crank them even higher, were the guitar heroes.

They also loved feedback. First one would feed back, then all of them would be feeding back madly until the song disappeared beneath these torrents of noise. It was like someone tossing a bloody chicken into a school of piranha.

KREUTZMANN
*and I worked hard
at synchronizing our
drumming. I taught
Billy what I knew of
the rudiments, and
he taught me how
to rock.*

*Portrait of
a Drummer
at the Edge
of Noise*

139

Phil would be almost foaming at the mouth, throwing his guitar into his amp. And Jerry would just drop everything and run at his amp, as if he couldn't get back there to start feeding back fast enough. God, it was exciting. For a few minutes you'd be out on the edge with this roaring animal all around you and it was always an open question whether it was going to go back into its cage or not. Then someone would remember the song or start another one, and all the dangerous possibilities would evaporate.

This seemed to happen every other song in the early days. Pigpen hated it. This wasn't the blues. He would hide behind his organ, and we'd have to call him to come back out and play. In one sense I don't blame him. When it came to noise, we were like children, learning to walk. We were making our first tentative experiments in what has turned out to be a lifetime obsession with finding the perfect balance between clarity and volume.

Kreutzmann and I worked hard at synchronizing our drumming. Sometimes we'd play for hours with our arms around each other, Billy handling one drumstick, me the other. One of our most intense drum experiments occurred while we were making the album *Anthem of the Sun* in Los Angeles. The band had rented a former movie star's castle in the Hollywood Hills, an enormous, spooky building with damp concrete walls and winding staircases. Billy and I moved our drum pads into an empty room and stayed in there for days. Employing some intensive hypnotic techniques I had learned, Kreutzmann and I now attempted to lock up at a deep level. We'd play for hours: I taught Billy what I knew of the rudiments, and he taught me how to rock.

I had heard, of course, of the phenomenon of rhythmic entrainment that rock and jazz musicians call "the groove." I had even fleetingly experienced it, but Billy taught me to trust in it, to let it draw me in like a tractor beam.

Something happened during those weeks in Los Angeles that was almost physical. It was as if Kreutzmann and I had learned how to synchronize our hearts, how to bond that basic physiological beat, so that, even though our styles of drumming were very different, there was now a rhythm linking us when we played.

Drumming at the Edge of Magic

140

THE ORIGINAL GRATEFUL DEAD HOUSE WAS AT 710 ASHBURY, BUT BY the time I arrived on the scene Kreutzmann and Lesh had rented the bottom floor of a house on Belvedere Street, a few blocks away. There was a small closet in this apartment, little-used because it had been built under a stairwell that ran through it to the floor above. This became my room. It was big enough for a mattress and a candle. I holed up in there for hours, beating on my drum pad to records that I played over and over again on a little portable stereo.

One day Phil handed me a record and said, "I think you should hear this!" It was called *Drums of North and South India,* and featured a master tabla player named Alla Rakha. I'd been fooling around with a pair of tablas without really knowing what I was doing, so I was pretty excited as I slipped the record onto my turntable and picked up the tablas, ready to mimic the beat.

I may have tapped the skins two or three times as the record started, but no more than that. I remember sitting there, totally dumbfounded, feeling as if someone had turned the lights out. In terms of rhythm, I mean. It sounded like five or six guys playing these tight muscular rhythmic cycles that constantly changed. Every time I thought I had the beat nailed, it would evaporate, only to pop up a minute later as a completely new rhythm. It was like chasing a greased pig blindfolded. I grabbed the record jacket. No way this could be one middle-aged Indian. But that's what the liner notes said.

I opened the door and yelled for Phil. "Do me a favor," I said. "Read the back of this album and tell me that this is just one guy playing." Phil assured me it was.

Alla Rakha was a rhythm master — my first. He was a Mozart of my instrument, an Einstein of rhythm, and yet world music was arranged into such a rigid caste system that I had never heard of this man. Nor had anyone ever told me that in India drummers had refined the art of rhythm to such a sublime complexity that it sounded, even to someone who had been working with it all his life, like magic.

Several weeks later, the Grateful Dead were off to New York City to play Bill Graham's Fillmore East. The first night at the Fillmore there were almost more people backstage than in the audience. One of them was a woman named Jean Mayo, who was in New York chaperoning the first American tour of a classical Indian troupe that included sitarist Ravi Shankar and drummer Alla Rakha. They were playing in Mineola, Long Island, on one of my free nights.

ALLA RAKHA
*was a rhythm master —
my first. Rakha
(left) and his son
Zakir Hussain.*

Seeing Alla Rakha play was like having a divine wish granted. The whole time he performed my eyes were locked on his hands. I didn't even have a good sense of what he looked like until Jean introduced us later backstage.

Learning that I was a drummer, Alla Rakha invited me back to his hotel room for tea. I brought my pad and sticks with me, and I also happened to bring along a curious little device known as a trinome. A trinome is a metronome that can keep track of three rhythmic cycles. Each cycle has a different sound. You can set it so the three beats will all weave in and out of one another, circling around in endless loops, and every time the loops intersect with one another a bell will bong, indicating what is known as "the One."

The One – the alpha and the omega, the beginning and the end of the rhythmic cycle.

Alla Rakha was amused by the trinome. Picking up my pad, he began to demonstrate a rhythm game to me. He beat out a count of ten and then called out a number, which I then tried to place on top of his next ten beats. For instance, when he called "twelve," I tried to lay twelve beats down within the span of his ten, so that his last beat and my last beat would meet – at the One. With this simple game, Alla Rakha destroyed my beliefs about rhythm. *Rhythm is just time, and time can be carved up any way you want.* We played eleven over nine and twelve over eight and fifteen over thirteen. He showed me the obvious truth that twelve bars of eleven are the same as eleven bars of twelve.

He held my hand as I beat so I could feel how time was utterly elastic. He made me feel what four felt like, then while I was doing four with my left hand, he showed me how I could put five into that four with my right hand.

Even beating on the pad with my fingers I felt it. Every time I crossed at the One, the energy shot up a little. There was a little *pop!* of something like adrenaline, only in my head. I returned from that hotel room feeling as if I'd been shown the Golden Tablets.

Back in San Francisco the Grateful Dead began playing Alla Rakha's rhythm games as a group. For months we spent all day, every day, except when there was a show, practicing, just laying sevens over fives and elevens over nines. Our song called "The Eleven," which explores a rhythmic cycle of eleven beats, dates from this period.

We felt we were on the edge of a breakthrough, that somewhere in these rhythm games was the key to a new kind of music – polyrhythmic rock and roll. It was during these months of experimentation that we ceased being a blues band and began mutating into our present form.

A lot of these rhythms couldn't be married to the backbeat, but some mated pretty well; even when the rhythmic match went nowhere, there was always the One. Every time we hit the One we got a little higher; the group groove grew a little deeper. Sometimes I felt we were becoming a big noisy animal that made music when it breathed.

We were also getting louder. That was another of our missions, to explore the edges of the sound envelope. We eventually spent millions trying to find a way to deliver the Grateful Dead sound clearly and accurately to the ears of our listeners, with volume but no distortion.

However, we also discovered that with each upgrade in volume, depths and subcurrents appeared in the music that we had never heard before, forcing us to readdress the way we dealt with the overall movement of the music. As the sound systems got bigger, we discovered that we could bounce our sound off the back of the arena and gauge what we sounded like from the audience's perspective. Possessing that information allowed us to manipulate the echo to deepen the audience's rhythmic involvement.

AFTER JOINING THE GRATEFUL DEAD, I RARELY SAW MY FATHER. WITH his newest wife he'd become a serious Christian. To him we were a bunch of freaks who played unlistenable music. But as we persevered and began to become successful, Lenny started coming around, hanging out. The drum store was going downhill; he was bored with it.

Since one of our grievous problems as a band was managing our money — we just couldn't seem to put together the business end of things in a way that worked — it was probably inevitable that Lenny's name would surface as a possible business manager. He'd been a banker, he'd run a music store, he'd been a player, and best of all he was the father of one of the band members. What more could people who hated the business side of music ask for? The hope was that Lenny would lead the Grateful Dead out into the light of twentieth-century financial wisdom.

He robbed us blind.

One night in 1970 some guys came on stage after a show to reclaim Pigpen's organ. We were stunned. From our perspective we were doing really well, playing nearly every night to one or two thousand people. The next day Phil and I went to see Lenny. Phil asked to see the books. Lenny refused in a suave, bankerly sort of way and at that instant I knew: he had stolen our money. While we had been struggling on this incredible adventure in sound sharing, my charming dad had been skimming off everything. How much he took, we could never discover.

Lenny went to jail for it. I couldn't go anywhere near him or the trial. I didn't want to play, didn't want to go out on the road. Confused, unbalanced, I wanted to flee and hide, bury my head and cry. I stopped touring with the Grateful Dead in 1971 and went to ground at the Barn.

I HAD FIRST MOVED OUT OF THE CITY TO THE NOVATO RANCH IN 1968. I had heard that the ranch had once belonged to the mistress of a wealthy Los Angeles doctor who, between visits from her lover, had avidly pursued her hobby, horticulture. Overgrown but still impressive herb and flower gardens covered about five acres of the grounds, with specimens from all around the world, and a sophisticated underground irrigation system to keep them healthy.

The ranch was communal, and even though I was no longer playing in the band, a large percentage of the extended Grateful Dead family lived there at one time or another. Though I was the ostensible host, most of the time I was deep into solitude and was allowed to live unhindered with my pain. The band didn't blame me for Lenny's thievery; they made that clear. They even kept paying me, treating my departure as a leave of absence that would end whenever I managed to pin to the ground the demons I was wrestling. Whenever I was ready, I was welcome back.

Three years would pass. Looking back, it was like an atonement. Having spent three years going deeper into volume and noise, I was now sentenced to three years of silence and noise — the noise of insects singing in the gardens at night, the trees creaking in the wind. I was a kid of concrete streets and sixty-cycle electrical lines and industrial urban noise. I found myself listening to the rhythms of nature.

Particularly water. I'd never thought much about water, about where it came from, how vital it is to life. At the ranch I was learning the simple, natural fact that you can't have an oasis without water; you can't have culture without water. There's a reason why civilization is riverine, springing up in the Indus, Nile, and Tigris-Euphrates valleys.

The heartbeat of the ranch was the pump – this gurgling throb of water. When it was on, you felt safe; when it was off, you were never without a slight, nagging worry. A broken pump was not such a rare occurrence as we might have hoped, and it meant an immediate reordering of priorities.

The longer I lived at the ranch, the more attuned I became to the pump's song. A part of my brain was always on, scanning for that distinctive sound, even when I slept. In fact, one of my first attempts at musical composition was a song built around the rhythm of the pump; it later received the title, "The Greatest Story Ever Told."

One day Joe Smith, the president of Warner Bros. records, came to the Barn to see me. There had been some discussion of a solo record and as I had refused to visit him in Los Angeles, he had been forced to enter my zone. He arrived in an enormous black limousine. It looked as if some futuristic insect had landed in our humble rural yard.

Joe was so nervous. I realized later that he had probably heard all kinds of disturbing tales about our commune in the hills north of San Francisco. This was noise for him; this was the edge. But it was precisely out of strange zones like this that new music was coming.

He loosened up by the minute and by the end was starting to get jovial. I talked about rhythm and noise and about a theory I had concerning the mixing of environmental sounds – water, crickets – with a steady rock backbeat. Environmental rock. I played him the pump song as an example of what I was up to. Joe loved it. By the time he got back into his limo, I had a contract for three records. And more important, I had the money to build a good studio. For the first time I was going to have unlimited time in which to push deeper and deeper into musical space.

My desire for a sixteen-track studio, the state of the art at the time, had been growing intense. Within the music business, the tradition had been that the two sides – engineers and artists – rarely mixed. The engineers tended to be these surly old guys who scowled and growled whenever you got too close to their switches. And the artists were too busy being artistes to dirty their hands with stuff that was more science than art.

I STOPPED *touring with the Grateful Dead in 1971 and went to ground at the Barn.*

One of the people who passed through the ranch about this time was Stephen Stills. Stephen had about twenty-five guitars, set to different open tunings scattered all over the Barn. Wherever he went, he could pick up another guitar tuned to a different modality. He used to play for hours on his guitar orchestra and at times I would join in on my hand drums. One day I saw Stephen sit down at the control board of a studio and play it like one of his guitars. Here was somebody who was my age, in my business, who had understood that rock and roll was electronic music and the technology was an inseparable extension of the instrument. Watching Stephen I realized that unless I knew as much about the electronic recording end of music as I did about the playing, I would never be in control of my musical destiny.

Around this time I acquired my first stereo Nagra and began running around the Bay Area with Dan Healy, the Grateful Dead's sound engineer, taping unusual music. We recorded all the early Indian classicists who arrived in Alla Rakha's and Ravi Shankar's wake — masters of the sarod, the sitar, the tabla. I loved rolling tape. At night I'd play back my tapes and sit in the darkened Barn, sipping cognac. It was one of my greatest pleasures.

One day Alla Rakha appeared at the Barn. He had a young boy with him, his eighteen-year-old son Zakir. Zakir was going to teach tabla at Ali Akbar Khan's school of music in Berkeley. Alla Rakha asked whether his son could stay with me.

"You and my son are of the same generation," he said. "I know you will get along. You can play with each other, teach each other, become brothers of the drum."

I told him his son could stay as long as he wanted.

ZAKIR,
*like his father, was a
genius on the tabla.*

So much context was missing from that first meeting. I didn't know then that Alla Rakha was also Zakir's teacher. Or that Zakir, like his father, was a genius on the tabla, that one day he would revolutionize tabla playing by loosening up the strict rhythmic cycles. I didn't know that I'd invited a young rhythm master into my life until the day he told me his story:

THE YOUNG RHYTHM MASTER'S TALE

When my father was eleven years old he had a dream in which he saw a strange face and heard the words, "Go to this person."

My father lived in Paghwal, in Punjab. Shortly after this dream he ran away from home. He went to the nearest big town and asked where he could go to study music. People referred him to a teacher.

When he arrived at this teacher's house and the man opened the door, my father saw it was the face of the man in his dream.

The teacher said, "What do you want?"

"I want to play tabla," answered my father.

The teacher took his own tabla and sat down to play. He told my father to sit in front of him and asked him to put his hands on another set of tabla. When the teacher looked up, he saw that my father was holding the drum the same way he was. Everything was identical, finger positions, hands, everything. They were connected in the spirit zone.

My father began to study rhythm with this teacher. He lived in his guru's house and did the errands, the cooking, the washing. Musicians were always coming to visit his teacher. My father would make tea for them, then retire to a corner to watch and listen. The main lessons my father learned were respect for his teacher and dedication to the art of the tabla.

Often the teacher was busy. Weeks would pass and he wouldn't spend any time with my father, being busy with concerts or other students. But then he'd sit down with my father and for two or three days they'd do nothing but play tabla together.

In time, and with much practice, my father became a master.

I was born the first son following three daughters, which in India can be a sign of bad luck. At the time of my birth, my father was dying of a heart ailment, and my mother, distraught by what seemed to be her husband's impending death, refused to nurse me. I was given to my mother's best friend who took me home and nursed me.

When I was a few weeks old, I was taken to see my father. As soon as I was placed in his arms, the dying man opened his eyes. Somehow he knew I was his son. Putting his lips by my ear he began to sing the drum syllables: "Te-ri-ki-ta, te-ri-ki-ta, te-ri-ki-ta."

A wandering holy man, a *sadhu,* happened to be passing by and he stopped at our home. "Look after this baby," he told my mother, "because he is going to make your husband better. Your husband is going to live."

"What do you mean?" my mother asked.

"For the next four years of his life you must guard him," the holy man continued, "because this child will be close to death many times. You have to guard him."

And it was as the holy man predicted. For the next four years I was close to death many times. Boils erupted on my body; once I nearly died from drinking kerosene, to say nothing of the usual viruses and plagues, most of which I got. The curious thing, though, was that the sicker I got, the better my father became.

He became my teacher when I was seven. I used to get up at one o'clock in the morning because that was when my father got home from his concerts. The house would be dark. We'd sit in the quiet and I'd massage my father's legs and arms, while he talked to me about music.

There was much more talk than playing. But every so often my father would give me a rhythm lesson. He'd say, "Okay, here's a little phrase that ends on four and a half. Now how are you going to make this little phrase fit into a cycle of sixteen beats." At that time of the morning!

One of the reasons my father picked the late night for my lessons was because musicians in India were night people and had to learn to get by on very little sleep. Traditional performances, particularly in private homes, would start at nine o'clock at night and often go until five or six in the morning.

When I turned eleven I began accompanying my father. This meant that on concert nights I got very little sleep, since I had to go to school the next morning at 7:30. But I wanted to do it. I looked forward to being woken up every night. I would cry if I was not taken to a concert with him. I would even insist that I be allowed to sit on the stage with him, though well back out of sight, so I could watch his hands, see how he approached the tabla, how he interacted with the person he was playing with.

I was my father's shadow.

When I was seventeen I went on my first *chilla,* which is a ritual retreat. A musician is supposed to do three of them. A hut is prepared for you in a remote region, usually near the village of your guru's ancestors. For forty days you live in that hut, doing nothing but playing music.

The first one I did I thought would be easy. I bathed, recited the proper mantras, and then played my instrument for fifteen hours. A breeze. A drummer can take one rhythmic cycle, or *tal,* per day, or just play one *tal* for forty days.

By the second day the vibrations of the constant drumming were beginning to work on my consciousness. I saw things in the music that I'd never seen before, new combinations, new patterns. By the third day, however, I was starting to get bored. By the morning of the fourth day I did not want to touch my tabla. I forced myself to play.

From the fifth day on I have little memory. I don't remember when I took a bath or ate. As soon as I began playing the visions would start. Everyone who does a *chilla* has these visions. They are an extension of the emotions, so that if I felt good, then the visions would be good. I'd heard stories of people who had had many bad experiences in life and when they went to do *chillas* their hallucinations were so scary that they screamed – and the *chilla* was broken.

On the twelfth day, my father appeared to me. He was there beside me. I could hear his voice saying, "Don't do it like that, do it like this. This is the way to do it. Okay, now try this combination."

I don't know how many days my father sat there with me, but eventually he changed into a very old, sagelike person. He was still my father, but now he had a long white beard and wrinkled skin, and eyes that were strangely radiant. "Do this, do that, try this combination," said the new vision.

I would have kept playing in this trance state perhaps forever if my father hadn't come to bring me home at the end of the fortieth day. I ached, I could barely walk, my eyes were big staring hollows.

I recuperated for two days, then my father asked me what I'd seen.

"I saw you teaching me," I said.

"I wasn't there but I was thinking of you a lot."

"And I saw a very old man."

My father asked me to describe him and when I did he said, "I believe that is your great grand-guru, Kader Baksh, who was my teacher's teacher. The way you've described his face, it sounds just like the way my teacher described him."

A CHILLA
*is a ritual retreat –
for forty days you
do nothing but
play music.*

That was the end of my first *chilla*. Six months later I had a second *chilla*. My father protested that it was much too soon, but I was adamant and I arranged things myself.

The first ten days were like before, though now I was expecting the visions. On the eleventh day, however, something strange happened. My tabla changed shape. It became a different instrument. It looked like a cross between a tabla and a big conga drum, except it also had eyes and a mouth, and it started talking to me.

I was afraid of this drum. It scared me. Suddenly my father appeared, as he had during my first *chilla,* only this time he was agitated.

"What are you doing?" he cried. "Stop doing that! Do something else."

He tried to pull me away from the strange vision by reciting a new composition that he'd been working on. But I couldn't stop watching the talking drum. Suddenly it too disappeared and I had a momentary vision of myself playing for all these blonde people. I was here in the U.S., playing with Ravi Shankar and Ali Akbar Khan. Then that vision faded and the drum was back, chattering away at me.

It reappeared throughout the next thirty days, sometimes terrifying me, always fascinating me. "It's an instrument," I kept telling myself. "An instrument can't hurt me; it's just a musical instrument. Why would a musical instrument want to hurt me?"

I think my father must have sensed that something strange had happened during my second *chilla*. Maybe he even knew what it was. But he did not try to stop me from coming to America, which I had seen in my vision. When he saw I was determined to go, he arranged to come with me, and he brought me here to you.

It was clear to me that the drum in Zakir's hallucination was the backbeat talking to him. Indian drummers like Zakir and Alla Rakha had taken rhythmic complexity to its ultimate expression, but they often played like brilliant metronomes. I would say to him, "Zakir, relax, it's okay, it's the groove! Let it move you. Don't worry about being imprecise, sometimes that's what it takes to feel right."

Of course, the learning more often went the other way. In India a drummer, besides being rhythmically accurate, has to fuse with the other musicians to express the dominant emotion being conveyed by the *raga* they're playing, whether it's happiness, anger, sadness, disgust, love, or hate. Every musical tradition develops its shorthand way of feeding this emotional hunger, but the palette is a little different in each. One of the first things Zakir taught me was this Indian drum palette of emotional expression.

The second thing he gave me was Diga. Zakir had a rehearsal band made up of some of the best students at Ali Akbar Khan's school. When I joined them, they had been entertaining the notion for some time of creating a tuned percussion orchestra modeled after the gamelan orchestras of Bali. I took this notion, added to it my growing inventory of Western drums, a good PA system, and a taste of the backbeat, and in the course of the next few months we evolved into a fourteen-eyed monster of rhythm and noise.

We called ourselves the Diga Rhythm Band, after the sound one of the drums makes — "deee-ga." Practices were often held at the Barn, particularly after we began exploring the dynamics of marathon sessions. We knew that Indian musicians frequently played all night — dusk to dawn — and as we got more proficient we decided, as an endurance test, to do an all-nighter. The first time we tried this we found ourselves in a full-blown, sound-sharing trance. A common pulse emerged, fed by an endless stream of rhythms that flowed out of our instruments, seemingly without conscious effort.

Where the number four came from I don't remember, but gradually a plan formed and grew beautifully irresistible that we should hold a mini-*chilla;* four days and nights of nothing but Diga. Stocks of food were laid in and sleeping bags were piled in the corner of the Barn. The idea was never to let the beat of the drum die. For the next four days at least two of us would be playing at all times.

I remember duos and trios and quartets and occasionally the full band. I remember people taking their instruments to the bathroom. I remember playing what seemed like brilliant compositions, except there was no time to either marvel at or judge the effects of the sounds we were making. They were like smoke drifting away on the breeze, fed by a constant flame of rhythm. I remember drifting and playing for hours, playing for so long that my hands finally couldn't move, and then falling asleep with my instrument.

What I don't remember is playing for four days, but friends tell me we did.

WE CALLED
*ourselves the Diga
Rhythm Band, after
the sound one of the
drums makes —
"deee-ga."*

MY LIFE BECAME INTENSELY QUIET IN A WAY THAT HAD NOTHING TO do with solitude. Far from the din of rock and roll, I came to understand that everything made sounds, that the world was composed of rhythms that could be read in stirrings as subtle as the movements of the insects, the shifting of the breezes.

Wandering the ranch, or riding a horse, or standing in the garden at night in the rain, I sometimes experienced moments of profound effortlessness, enormous natural grooves that on a good day could carry me for hours. I was opening to the animal powers, to what Rolling Thunder called the spirit side.

His Western name was John Pope and his Western job was working as a brakeman for the railroad. His Indian name was Rolling Thunder and his Indian job was medicine man.

Rolling Thunder entered the scene during that brief intermixing of counterculture and Native American culture that had taken place in the early days of the Haight-Ashbury, becoming intertwined with members of the Grateful Dead extended family, many of whom called upon his services when they were sick. The ranch became his base whenever he was in the Bay Area; he did his curing there, replenishing his medicinal herbs, his yellow dock and his sage, from the overgrown herb gardens.

When Rolling Thunder was in residence, one of his sons would rise at dawn and wake the place with a barking cry.

Hooowwwwwooooohhh.

A fire would be built on a little hill near the Barn, and everyone would gather there before breakfast. We would sing songs, accompanied on the drum by a couple of people from Rolling Thunder's entourage – he usually traveled with five or six young Indians, sons and apprentices – who drummed a steady, hypnotic rhythm. Rolling Thunder would then call on the four winds to carry our morning prayers up with the smoke, then he would hand everyone the tobacco, which would be tossed into the fire.

After this solemn ceremony, people who were new to the ranch would be welcomed. We'd talk about community problems, about who might be in trouble or in need, or about this or that significant event that had happened recently. Rolling Thunder had a rap, a sort of sermon. He was not an apolitical man; he wanted justice for the Native Americans, and he was rightfully bitter about their collective mistreatment at the white man's hands. But he was far angrier and sadder about the Western white man's wholesale destruction of the environment. Rolling Thunder wanted the animals to return to the earth; he was a prophet for the animal powers. Everything in nature has a spirit, he told us over and over again. Nature is alive. But if you don't respect its life, then it can die.

I didn't recognize who he was at the time. His drumming and rattling, his speeches about the spirits of nature — it would be years before I would connect Rolling Thunder with the shamanic tradition that stretched back in an unbroken line to the deep Paleolithic.

I saw Rolling Thunder perform many healings. He was a sucker and a sniffer, in the sense that he would move all around the sick person's body, sniffing for the poison, making animal cries and chanting, while one of his apprentices drummed and rattled. When he located the source of the poison, Rolling Thunder would suck it out, spitting it into a pail. Then he would take an eagle feather — the eagle was one of his animal allies — and carefully clean the sick person with it, running the feather over the body and depositing whatever bad energy it absorbed into a piece of meat, which was then burned in the fire. Finally, the sick person would be cleansed with smoke from the smudge pot and Rolling Thunder would prescribe herbs.

After a healing Rolling Thunder would go somewhere to be alone. Once I followed him when he wandered into the woods around the Barn. He was like a drunk person, grabbing onto trees and throwing up. This, I realized, was the price he paid for his gift. Every time Rolling Thunder healed someone, he willingly poisoned himself. He was walking the razor's edge, absorbing the bad energy into his body because he had been chosen and schooled in the ancient techniques that taught you not just how to find and suck out the badness, but then how to purge it from your own body as well. The day Rolling Thunder lost the power to perform this last crucial task would be the day he would start to die.

ROLLING THUNDER

was a prophet for the animal powers.

Portrait of a Drummer at the Edge of Noise
159

FOR THREE YEARS I HAD TUNED OUT ALL NEWS OF THE GRATEFUL Dead, but now I became aware that while I had been drifting in my own pool of solitude, the band had been slipping into crisis. The rumors swirling around the ranch had them breaking up, quitting touring. Supposedly they were going to play a farewell set at Winterland in October 1974, five days of Grateful Dead music, and then the plug would be pulled.

The more I contemplated this impending conclusion to what had been the most exciting musical experience of my life, the more I realized that I wanted desperately to play Grateful Dead music one more time.

On the night of the last concert I packed my drums into my truck and drove to Winterland, arriving at the break between sets. I asked Ram Rod to set up my drums on stage and then went to look for the guys. They were in the dressing room, happy to see me arrive. It was appropriate that we'd all be here together at the end.

I was back on the bus, for however long there was going to be a bus.

CHAPTER TEN

Shaman's Drum: Skeleton Key To The Other Worlds

IF YOU HAD ASKED ME A few years ago to define a shaman, I would have said that the word meant fake or sham. I thought shamans were like stage magicians, using all sorts of tricks and ventriloquism to fool people into believing they had special powers. Now I know better. As I discovered from my readings, the word *shaman* comes from the culture of the pastoral herding peoples of the Asian steppes, where it is used to describe individuals in the tribe who can enter into a trance in order to commune with the spirit world.

161

FOR THE
*shaman, the drum
is not so much a
musical instrument
as a vehicle for
transportation.*

Joseph Campbell thought shamans were probably the first spiritual figures we had, the first mystics. He also thought it likely that they were the first artists, the first musicians, and the first storytellers, mainly because whenever you asked contemporary shamans to describe what they experienced in the trance state, the stories they told had the same resonant mysterious quality as the myths Joe loved.

Were myths merely the stories the first shamans learned in that shadow realm, in that other world the mystics say surrounds and blends with this one? Joe thought it likely, and so do I, though to be perfectly honest, what first caught my attention with regard to shamans were their drums.

Shamans are drummers — they're rhythmists, they're trance masters who have understood something fundamental about the nature of the drum, something I badly wanted to learn.

I noticed, as I began to study the anthropological debate over percussion and transition, that most of the examples of percussive trance fell into two broad categories. In the first, drumming was used to summon the spirits or the gods down into the body of someone other than the drummer, usually a dancer. This is known as possession trance. The classic example is vôdun, where the spirits — called the *loa* — are said to descend and mount the bodies of the dancers and ride them like horses.

The second type of trance is shamanic or "communion trance," the opposite of possession trance in almost every way. In a communion trance the spirit or soul of the drummer is said to ride his drumbeat like a horse up to the spirit world, where he (and it is usually a male) transacts his business in an active rather than a passive way.

Possession trance is usually found among agricultural peoples — people whose spiritual life is rooted in the earth — while the communion trance is strongly associated with hunters and gatherers, nomads, and herders — wandering people for whom the sky is the source of the sacred. Possession trance captivated the Western imagination early on, so there is considerable literature on it. It's only recently, however, that shamanism has begun to get the attention it deserves. The scholarly bible is probably Mircea Eliade's *Shamanism: Archaic Techniques of Ecstasy,* though many more people have been introduced to shamanism via books like Michael Harner's *The Way of the Shaman.* Eliade calls shamans "technicians of ecstasy." What this means is that shamans are people who have developed techniques that allow them to enter esoteric states of consciousness. In modern psychological jargon, they are individuals who have mastered lucid dreaming, clairvoyance, clairsentience, out-of-the-body travel – the whole spectrum of what psychiatrist Stan Grof calls "nonordinary states of consciousness." Shamans can be thought of as individuals who have learned how consciously to enter some of these states and then bring back to this reality the information they obtain there.

They do this primarily to serve their community, their consciousness roaming far beyond the fires of the human body, keeping watch over those who cannot traffic in the spirit world. Shamans are healers and weatherworkers; they lobby the spirits to ensure a good hunt; they keep a watch on the future and are capable of tapping into the deep past. The Yahgan people, who live off the coast of Chile, tell of a time when food was scarce because of stormy weather. They asked their shaman for help. He went into a trance and when he emerged from it he told them to go west along the southern shore of the channel until they came to a place where two whales were beached on the sand. The whales were pregnant, he said, and had been driven ashore by a killer whale. And it was as he said.

In Australia the aboriginal shamans are weathermakers and healers, although there is a special class of supershaman known as a *munkumbole* whose speciality is clairvoyance. Once or twice a year, on the new moon, all the *munkumbole*s meet to compare and discuss visions and work out the future path of their people.

Shamans rarely inherit their special place within these societies, although you do find families where the disposition carries through several generations; shamans are usually discovered, then refined. The role of shaman has often been thought to favor the flawed, the weak, the crippled, the outcast; it does, however, take a healthy, rather robust mind to go into trance, with ease, on a regular basis. People of different ethnic groups distinguish very well between those who are mentally ill and those who are shamans.

In Mexico a young boy is bitten by a snake and lies paralyzed for months. His grandfather, a shaman, predicts that if he lives he will become a great shaman. Among the Ainu of Japan, a woman falls ill with a traditional female nervous disease called *imi,* which manifests itself variously as eye trouble, arthritis, or functional paralysis. If she succeeds in curing herself – that is, drives the bad spirit from her body – then a good spirit will come to live near her. The spirit might be that of a snake, a fox, or a caterpillar. When the woman enters a trance state, this spirit will speak to her and tell her the nature of the illnesses of those who now come to her to be cured.

General rule number one: shamans are often those who have cured themselves, and in the process have discovered the knowledge that now allows them to cure others.

AMONG THE YAHGAN IT OFTEN HAPPENS IN THE WOODS OR AT THE shore. A man might be walking in the woods and suddenly a tree spirit will jump out and confront him. Or a woman might be loitering at the beach and a large fish will swim in close to shore and gaze at her. Or, most powerfully, she might be safely at home sleeping, when the giant whale that has visited her people for so many generations comes rising into her innocent dreams.

These are not casual visitations for the young Yahgan, since they result in a state of semitrance that draws the attention of the older shamans. The older shamans wait until there are enough potential shamans to warrant convening a school.

When enough potential shamans have appeared, the older shamans build a conical wooden hut. Teachers and students will live in this hut, not venturing out for several months, existing on starvation rations. Although women are allowed to attend the school, they are often regarded as lesser vessels in terms of shamanic power. Everyone must be chaste, and silence prevails until noon. One of the first rituals the students undertake is the rubbing off of their old skin, so a more sensitive skin can grow over their body. The older shamans warm their hands over the fire and then pour the warmth over the students, who are naked during their whole initiation. The warmth of the fire is said to burn away the fog from the novices' eyes, so they can see their spirit allies and learn the songs they are supposed to sing to them.

General rule number two: shamans are people who can see the spirits, both good and bad, and manipulate them accordingly.

THE INITIATION OF THE YOUNG YAHGAN SHAMANS IS BENEVOLENT and collegial compared to the ordeal that an Inuit must face. In the case of a boy named Igjugarjuk, it was a series of compelling dreams that alerted the tribe that the "mysterious divine force Sila" had chosen him to become shaman.

An older shaman was designated his instructor. He loaded Igjugarjuk onto a dogsled and took him out into the wintry vastness of the Canadian arctic. After traveling for some miles, the old shaman stopped and proceeded to build a tiny snow hut that was barely big enough for the boy to sit cross-legged in. On the floor of the hut the shaman placed an animal pelt. Then he lifted Igjugarjuk from the sled and carried him into the snow hut, careful that at no time did his feet touch the snow. He placed the boy on the animal skin and then left, telling Igjugarjuk to focus all his attention on the Great Spirit, who would hear his call and come to protect him.

For five days Igjugarjuk sat there without food or water. At the end of the fifth day his teacher arrived and gave him a small drink of water, then departed. He returned at the end of the fifteenth day and gave the boy a small piece of meat. At the end of the thirtieth day he took Igjugarjuk home. The Great Spirit had protected the boy; he had become a shaman. Describing his initiation years later, Igjugarjuk observed that the strain on his body had been so intense that it felt like "sometimes it died a little."

General rule number three: a shaman is someone who has undergone a symbolic death and been reborn into a higher integration. In order to accomplish this symbolic death it is often necessary to actually bring the body to a point approaching death, thus allowing the spirits to gain a foothold. Only after the body has been weakened and the spirit world contacted, does the shaman become able to leave the body and go adventuring up and down the World Tree.

WITHIN THE LITERATURE OF WESTERN MYSTICISM, THOSE ZONES of nonordinary consciousness that surround us are frequently called "the other world." Descriptions of what this spiritual geography is like vary according to culture. Aldous Huxley, who found his way to the other world using psychedelics, described it as "the Antipodes of the mind. In this psychological equivalent of Australia we discover the equivalents of kangaroos, wallabies, and duck-billed platypuses – a whole host of extremely improbable animals, which nevertheless exist and can be observed."

For the shaman the other world is shaped like a tree, the World Tree. Beating a drum or shaking a rattle, a shaman sings the songs that alert his spirit allies that they are needed. His trance deepens until his soul slips out of his body and flies across the world to the Tree that stands at the center of the universe. Then he begins to climb. If he goes up into the branches toward the leaves, his destination is the heavens, culminating in the Lord of the Universe. If he goes down into the roots of the World Tree, then his destination is the underworld.

The Apache shaman Geronimo described the journey this way: "As I sing, I go through the air to a holy place where Yusun [the Lord of the Universe] will give me power to do wonderful things. I am surrounded by little clouds, and as I go through the air I change, becoming spirit only."

Sometimes the shaman transforms into a wolf, an eagle, a bear, a fish, a reindeer, or some other animal form to make the trip; sometimes his soul remains intact and he travels with a spirit entourage, consulting them on strategy. In cases of healing, the shaman often sends one of his allies to retrieve the errant soul of the sick member of the tribe, which is seen as wandering aimlessly outside the body.

Far from being a private, solitary act, this ecstatic transformation is undertaken in full view of members of the community. Their presence is as necessary to the successful completion of the shamanic journey as is the shaman's ability to enter trance and find the World Tree.

SOME WONDERFUL DESCRIPTIONS OF SHAMANIC PERFORMANCE LIE buried in the anthropological literature, and as I read more deeply, I could see and hear the shamanic performance come alive. The one that most vividly sticks in my mind concerns an Evenk shaman who has been called upon to heal an ailing man in his village. The Evenk were a pastoral people who lived in Siberia, and their shamanic performances took place in a round tent that was carefully decorated to distinguish it as a ritual space connecting this world and the timeless one of the spirit.

The east side of the tent represents the upper world. Several large wooden figures hang there, images of the giant reindeer who are the Evenk shaman's most powerful spirit allies. Slightly south of these figures is a pole containing numerous swatches of colored fabric and animal skins. This pole represents the road to the upper deities — the sun, the moon, and assorted others, which are known collectively to the Evenk as "Bear."

The west side of the tent is the way to the underworld. Again numerous figures are placed there to represent the spirit allies the shaman will use to travel below, in this case the elk and the stag. In the center of the tent is a tall larch tree, the World Tree.

When the ritual is about to begin, the shaman picks up his drum, warms it over the fire to give the skin its proper tension, and then sits down with it on his left knee and strikes the rim with his drumstick. All conversation ceases.

The shaman begins his first song, an invocation to the spirits. After each verse, everyone present sings a rhythmic refrain. As the song progresses the shaman begins to call on his spirit allies. He names each of them and describes their power and the services they have rendered to the tribe. He tells how he sees them leaving their homes and coming to this isolated tent.

The drumming becomes softer and the song is interrupted by the sounds of the spirits, grunts and whistles, and the whirring of wings. As each spirit appears the shaman yawns deeply, swallowing his allies. Then the song changes. Orders are given to the various allies. Some are sent to guard the door; others watch the various pathways to the East and North, to make sure nothing unexpected happens to harm the shaman when he is in this vulnerable state.

Because the point of this performance is a healing, the shaman dispatches his chief ally down the World Tree to the underworld, where it seeks out the shaman's ancestor spirit who will tell it the nature of the man's illness. The dialogue between ancestor spirit and ally is heard by all since it comes out of the shaman's mouth in the form of screams, grunts, and yells.

The drumming grows thunderous. Suddenly the shaman leaps to his feet. He sways from side to side, bending low and straightening, then he "looses such a torrent of sound on the audience that it seems that everything is humming — the poles of the tent, even the buttons on those present."

Throwing his drum to his assistant, the shaman's song rises to a scream and he begins to dance, pantomiming the journey of his ally in the underworld. He whirls and spins, he foams at the mouth, then he drops down and lies like one stricken. He is in deep trance. Having joined his ally in the underworld, he is no longer in this time.

Urgently his assistant grabs the drum, warms it over the fire and begins to beat it vigorously, calling to the shaman not to get lost in that dangerous land. Look at the fire, he yells. Listen to the drum so you can find your way back!

The drum becomes louder and louder. Suddenly the shaman screams. He leaps to his feet and begins dancing for the return of his chief ally. Presumably he now knows the nature of the bad spirit that is causing his patient's sickness.

HUNTER. GATHERER. TOOLMAKER. SINGER. DANCER. STORYTELLER. Shaman. Those are our oldest occupations.

It fascinated me that one of the first and most crucial gifts of the spirit world to the shaman is a song. A !Kung woman, describing this transmission, told anthropologist Lorna Marshall that God had stood next to her and repeated the song over and over again until she could sing it perfectly. Another woman shaman, an Alaskan, told the explorer Knud Rasmussen that "songs were born in stillness while all endeavored to think of nothing but beautiful things. Then they take shape in the minds of men and rise up like bubbles from the depths of the sea, bubbles seeking the air in order to burst. This is how sacred songs are made."

I read in Eliade that the songs of shamans are supposed to be a lost language of the animals that everyone could speak a long time ago, while now only the shamans can contact the animal powers.

The shamanic dance is also imitative of the animal allies that the shaman commands, though the point of the dance is probably as much physical as aesthetic. The !Kung say that when the medicine within a medicine man becomes stimulated by a dance, "warmed by the fire and by the heat of the man's body, the man's spirit may leave him, causing his body to fall because there is nothing there to hold it up, and fly into the veld, where it seeks out the evil that is troubling people. Some medicine men in this way have seen the spirits of the dead, some have seen the great god. . . . One man's spirit rushed out into the veld where it came upon a pride of lions that had been troubling the people by their deafening roar at night. The man's spirit spoke with the lions, defied them, and ordered them away, and the lions did go."

In the depths of the great Paleolithic cave at Lascaux, there is an image of a bird-headed shaman in a trance, lying next to a wounded bull. It is probably an image of hunting magic, the shaman's spirit perhaps rushing out onto the great plains in search of the wandering herds.

Not only do the shamans receive their songs from the spirit world, but most of the instruments they play as well. According to the Warao of Venezuela, the gourd rattle they use in their rituals was obtained many years ago from the spirit of the South by an ancestral shaman: "During his visit he received the sacred fire rattle and was given instructions about the creation of channels of communication with the supernatural so that he and his kind might never lose contact with the gods of the cardinal directions."

The Warao shaman fills his gourd, which has been carefully prepared according to the ritual instructions of the spirit of the South, with quartz crystals that have been shamanically empowered and represent the shaman's spirit allies.

OUR EARLIEST IMAGE OF A MUSICIAN — THE MASKED FIGURE FROM THE cave at Les Trois Frères — is also an image of a working shaman, playing what appears to be a musical bow. The musical bow is still in use in some central Asian communities as an instrument of trance, but in most places its function has been replaced by the frame drum. When this transformation happened is not known, but it is likely that it occurred sometime during the Mesolithic. Linguistically, you can read the progression in certain central Asian dialects as the musical bow was slowly replaced by the drum. Among some tribes, like the Yuraks, the drum is still referred to as a "bow" or a "singing bow."

For the shaman, the drum is not so much a musical instrument as a vehicle for transportation. Most frequently in Siberia, it is characterized as a horse that the shaman rides to the World Tree, though it can also be a boat (with the drumstick becoming an oar) or a bow (with the drumstick doubling as the arrow).

The shaman's drum is said to be constructed from a splinter of the World Tree that the Lord of the Universe made available for this purpose, thus ensuring the shaman a magical connection with the World Tree. When the shaman dies, his drum is hung on a tree in the woods not far from his grave.

There are several wonderful descriptions in the ethnographic literature describing the making of a shaman's drum. I particularly like the story of the Khakass, a Turkish-speaking people who live in southcentral Russia.

The Khakass shaman does not make his own drum. In a trance he receives special instructions from the "masters of the holy mountain," which he then imparts to the members of his tribe who are responsible for building the drum. These instructions are precise and detailed and include the location of the tree that is to furnish the wood for the drum's body, how the animal that will furnish the skin is to be killed, what sort of design will be etched upon this skin, what sort of pendants are to be fastened to the drum, and how the handle is to be fashioned. It is vital that the wood for the body of the drum and the handle be procured in such a way that the trees that furnish them are unharmed. If the trees die, it is considered a very bad omen.

The Khakass make their shaman drums from crimson willow. A thin band, less than half an inch thick and about five inches wide, is shaved from the willow. It must be long enough so that when the two ends of the willow band are fastened with leather thongs, the resulting hoop will have a diameter of about thirty inches. Any splinters or shavings are gathered together and carefully buried. It is important that no one walk on these splinters, particularly no women.

On either side of the drum's handgrip, which comes from a birch tree, hang four bronze bells with iron rings as clappers, plus five metal cones and six curved iron plates, all arranged to clash together when the drum is shaken. These metal objects and pendants serve several functions. The bells are the shaman's messengers; they also help in the recitation of the songs. The cones are used to drive away the bad spirits from the body of the sick person; they also warn the shaman when a rival shaman is trying to damage him, that is, "devour his soul." The curved plates are called swords and they too are used to ward off hostile spirits. The drumskin is made from horsehide, which is stitched to the body with tendon.

The birch handgrip is called *mars,* meaning tiger, and it represents the master spirit of the drum. Six pairs of holes are drilled in the handgrip. These are the eyes of the tiger. It is through these eyes that the shaman's spirit allies enter and depart from the drum. When they are inside the drum, the shaman enjoys their power.

Once the drum has been fashioned, the process begins that will slowly awaken it as an instrument of power. Before anything else can happen the drum must be played by a young child for three days, right before bedtime. This "lightens" the drum. Next, the skin of the drum is decorated with symbols of the shaman's world map. The surface of the drumskin is divided into two parts, one representing the upper world, the other the lower world. Usually, the map of the lower world predominates. Figures are drawn on the skin: dogs, frogs, toads, bears, reindeer, snakes, lizards. These represent not only his allies, but familiar landmarks he will encounter while entranced.

Once the world map has been drawn, the shaman begins to play an active part in the drum's awakening. Entrancing himself, he begins seeking the soul of the animal whose skin now covers his drum. He searches in the animal's favorite grazing spots, even locates the place where the animal was born, and eventually he captures the wandering soul. Then the shaman prepares a banquet, slaughtering a white lamb and obtaining a birch tree, roots and all, which is erected at the banquet and decorated with rings and bands.

The shaman now takes up his new drum for the first time and examines it to make sure his instructions have been precisely followed. Then he goes into trance and rides to the World Tree to show his drum to the Lord of the Universe, who in turn makes sure that all his instructions have been carried out. If the drum is approved, then the Lord of the Universe assigns the shaman his animal allies. He also tells the shaman how many drums he will play in his lifetime, which is a measure of how long the shaman's powers will endure.

When the shaman's drum dies, so does the shaman's power, and frequently so does the shaman.

WHEN THE
*shaman's drum dies, so
does the shaman's
power, and frequently
so does the shaman.*

I WAS AWARE, AS I PURSUED MY RESEARCH INTO SHAMANISM, THAT most of the scholars writing on this subject were not drummers. They had never ridden a drum anywhere, had never played one to the point of trance. Although they acknowledged the drum's centrality in shamanic performance, few were able to bring a performer's view to the role that percussive sound or percussive rhythm might be playing in the maintenance and elaboration of that performance.

These were questions right up my alley; in a sense I'd been thinking about them since childhood, when I first discovered that playing a drum pad in the closet stimulated a feeling of lightness, happiness, timelessness. In another culture, my capacity to access these states might have resulted in my becoming a shaman. Instead of Jonesy, I might have drawn a teacher like Perqánâq, who guided Igjugarjuk through his ordeal in the snow hut. I might have been taught how to ride my drum not into the rock and roll groove, but out of my body to the World Tree, where the animal powers live. As it was, I had glimpses of these powers in the drums I'd collected, but until now I had never really understood what they were.

The World Tree was a map of consciousness that emerged in the Paleolithic, making it the oldest such map we have. When LSD was proliferating in the Haight, the map of consciousness that most people were following was of much later origin, either Hindu or Buddhist or occult or twentieth-century psychological. None of my friends talked about shamans, and yet that's what we were all trying to become, without knowing it. We were climbing around in the World Tree of consciousness like adolescents, intent only on the thrill that came from playing in these dangerous spaces so far above the ground.

And how could it have been otherwise? There was a community waiting to be healed, but there were no teachers — or very few — and there was no tradition of exploring these states. The tradition that we had inherited disavowed their existence, insisting that the tiny box of consciousness that we all inhabited was all there was. And yet 250 millionths of a gram of a powerful psychochemical suggested that when it came to the mind and its attendant powers, the science of the twentieth century was no closer to solving the riddle than the science of the Egyptians or ancient Greeks had been.

Of course, using drugs to access and manipulate these nonordinary states was not a modern discovery. Classical shamanism was no stranger to the potentials of botanical allies to amplify trance. Plants such as the vine *ayahuasca*, the psilocybin mushroom, and the fly agaric mushroom have long histories of

BEATING A
*drum or shaking a
rattle, a shaman sings
the songs that alert his
spirit allies that they
are needed.*

Shaman's
Drum:
Skeleton
Key to the
Other
Worlds
175

shamanic use. And because we in the West have a tradition of altering brain metabolism with drugs, we are perhaps more sympathetic to the claims of shamans who use botanicals than we are to shamans who simply beat on a piece of horsehide stretched upon a willow frame.

But how does a drum alter consciousness? That was the question I'd started with and now I thought I could see an answer shimmering beneath the data. My first thought had been that there was something unique in the sound. Andrew Neher had seemed right in his theory that percussive noise played loudly over time eventually overwhelmed the hearing apparatus and this played a large part in inducing trance. The shamanic ritual, held in a small, enclosed space, seemed designed to enhance these percussive effects. In addition, the loudness of the drums would also activate the adrenals, flooding the body with adrenaline.

But Gilbert Rouget also seemed right when he argued that trance was culturally determined, that the cues that put a shaman into trance were not the same as those of a San tribesman, and that to generalize a cause-and-effect relationship between drums and trance was too simplistic, particularly if you took a global view of trance.

It occurred to me that drums did not play a part in the shaman's original crisis. When Igjugarjuk was left out there in the snow and told to contact the spirit world, he wasn't given a drum with which to do it. The assumption was — and it seems to pertain in all the shamanic initiations — that the initial connection with the animal powers, the ability to enter deep trance and contact certain spirits, precedes any involvement with percussion. Drumming wasn't even the most important musical component of the shamanic performance, since the songs of the spirit allies were far more crucial.

So what was going on? The more I asked myself this question, the more I felt that I was chasing my shadow. How did the shamanic performance work? For myself, I know that it's possible to ride the rhythms of a drum until you fall into a state of receptivity that can be construed as the beginnings of trance. When I'm drumming, I like to get as close to this state as I can, yet I also know that I can't let myself go completely because if I do, my drumming will deteriorate and I will quickly lose the state. There have been many times when I've felt as if the drum has carried me to an open door into another world, yet if I let myself pass through that door I can no longer drum and that yanks me back. Perhaps this is why the shaman has an assistant who takes over drumming as the trance deepens.

When the shaman reaches that door, he sings his songs and the spirit allies come, often taking up abode in his drum, which is then transformed into a horse that carries the shaman to the World Tree. Statements like "the shaman rides his drum like a horse" seemed to me to be a way of saying that "the shaman entrains with the rhythm of the drum and it carries him deeper into trance." Percussive noise might be helpful in inducing trance, but it was rhythmic entrainment that enabled the shaman to actually move into this spirit world. It seemed significant to me that the assistant was there mainly to keep the drumbeat going while the shaman was entranced and to shout out warnings that the shaman must not "get lost in that dangerous land; listen to the drum so you can find your way back."

This, I think, is the drum's function. Its rhythms set up a ripple in time, ensuring that the shaman can find his way back from the timelessness that is mentioned in almost all accounts of the other world. The danger to the shaman who has ridden the drum out of his body is not so much being lost in space as being lost in time. In a sense the drum functions as an extension of the heart that is beating in the shaman's empty body, back here in human time.

An instrument of time travel. A beacon when he is out of his body.

YOU CAN GO *lower and deeper with the Beam than with anything else I know, descending into vibrations that are perceived less by the ear than felt as shockwaves throughout the body.*

CHAPTER ELEVEN

PORTRAIT OF A DRUMMER AT THE EDGE OF MAGIC

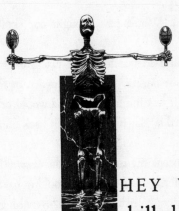

"THEY WERE SISTERS killed by an epidemic, that's what the dealer said. It's Tibetan, really old."

My friend pushed the little skull drum across the table, encouraging me to feel how easily the delicate crania fit the palm of my hand. I shook it tentatively.

Binnnggg . . . Gunnnggggg.

My friend leaned closer. "It's called a *damaru*. It's a power drum; only the most enlightened lamas have one of these. I just had to buy it for you when I spotted it. I knew you could appreciate its power."

179

When I had first met my friend, in the cheerful early months of the Haight, everyone had agreed that he was one of the most mystically savvy people in a place that was teeming with mystically savvy people. His rap on the Big Picture was one of the great ones.

I set the skull drum on the table, feeling a kind of creepy fascination. "Thanks, Bear."

Perhaps a week went by before I remembered the *damaru* and brought it out to play.

Binngggg . . . Gunnnngggg.

The sound was much bigger than I had expected. I examined the drum closely, noticing for the first time that the pieces of cloth that hung from it were decorated with exquisitely embroidered symbols. Someone had devoted a lot of time to the look of this drum.

Binngggg . . . Gunnnngggg.

That big sound again. Who'd have thought our skulls were so resonant?

Unfortunately, big sound seemed to be the extent of this *damaru*'s novelty; rhythmically it was quite boring. I played it for ten or fifteen more minutes before putting it away. It was fun to look at and would be fun to tell stories about, but I never expected to play it again. I set it back on a shelf and then went and threw up.

I had no reason to associate my nausea with the *damaru*. But I soon began bumping into things, falling down when I shouldn't have, injuring myself in minor but annoying ways; it gradually felt as if everything in my life was starting to unravel. It was only after several weeks of such uncharacteristic misfortune that I suddenly remembered the odd little Tibetan drum that Bear had given me. *It's a power drum!* And I remembered my friend's fondness for mystical jokes.

I tried playing the drum again but felt so awful that I telephoned psychologist Stanley Krippner and asked him to examine it. Krippner agreed with me about the *damaru*'s big sound and the unpleasant physical side effects, but he parried my suggestion that he take the drum with him for further study. I wanted the thing out of my house. Finally, I called bandmate Phil Lesh, explained the situation, and suggested that he might find Bear's gift interesting.

Phil took the drum off my hands, but two weeks later, the phone rang. It was Phil. "Mickey! I want you to come over and get this drum right now. I don't want it here another minute."

We sat at his table, drinking coffee and speculating on how we might honorably rid ourselves of this perverse instrument. Suddenly Phil said, "Why don't we give it back to the Tibetans."

Both of us had read in a recent article in the *San Francisco Chronicle* that the Tibetan Buddhists had opened a center in Berkeley, and one of the head lamas, Tarthang Tulku, was in town for the opening ceremonies. We grabbed the *damaru*, jumped into the car, and drove as quickly as we could to Berkeley. A golden-robed attendant ushered us inside, smiling benignly as we babbled on about needing to see his holiness on a matter of some urgency involving a drum.

After a few minutes' consultation among the monks, we were ushered into a room at the end of which Tarthang Tulku, an elegant little man, was sitting in a chair; an attendant was whispering the nature of our business. I walked forward and handed the head lama our *damaru*. He seemed to marvel at how comfortably the delicate crania fit his palm.

"So you've come home at last," he said, looking at the drum. Then he turned to me.

"I hope you have been most careful, Mickey Hart. This is a drum of great, great power. It wakes the dead, you know."

NOT LONG AFTER THIS, I DROVE MY CAR OVER A CLIFF. IT SNAGGED ON a tree halfway down, saving my life, but not all my bones.

Over the years I've entertained many interpretations of the lama's warning, the most obvious being that it referred to my impending car accident, to my sudden glimpse of my own mortality – the real Edge. But, as someone once pointed out to me, you could also interpret it as a reference to the Grateful Dead, since it was shortly after this that we returned to the studio and, for the first time in years, spent months just playing together and exploring, an adventure that produced our *Blues for Allah* album.

Lately I've come to focus more on the "waking up" and less on the "dead." It seems to me now that what the lama was telling me was that by playing the *damaru* I might have accidentally brought something back to life, I might have unwittingly opened the door for the spirits, and that is always risky.

But what door, what spirits?

My image of myself during that period is as a sort of human antenna swinging in the breeze, constantly scanning for musical information, completely absorbed in the endless symphony that was always playing in my head, my synethesia intensified by the fact that I was only seconds away from my studio.

Sunsets were an endless variation on a kind of red-gold tone that sounded to me like the tones you get from Tibetan bowls. Sometimes the sunsets were fuzzy, with a lot of humming overtones, and sometimes they had the clarity and serenity of a single ringing tone, very powerful, with a lot of body, lasting a whole orchestral movement. Whenever the rhythmic gurgling of the pump started, I'd hear my grandfather singing "Froggy Went a-Courtin'." Rain on the roof of the Barn became millions of soldiers on the march; it seemed to me that swarms of faces lived in the rain's harmonics, GI Joe types, stopping for smokes, resting awhile, then moving on, always marching, like some mythical army, coming in waves, disappearing in waves.

Everybody at the ranch was an explorer of one sort or another; my territory happened to be sound. I decorated the gardens with sounding objects of metal, glass, and bamboo. I hung wind chimes and metal strips in all the trees. It looked like a strange planet of percussion. Anything that made sound I listened to. I stood in the woods for long periods of time, my ear to the trunk of a tree, listening to its inner voice as it creaked in the wind, trying to push the edges of my sound envelope. I realized that everything must be making sound; the process of photosynthesis must be producing vibrations, if only we had sensitive enough ears. I began hearing the sacred in the noise.

Toward the end of this period I began to crave fire. Perhaps this was Rolling Thunder's influence, but fire filled me with a sense of deep, peaceful power. I started building fires at night and chanting around them, playing bullroarers and gongs. There was something about the outdoors, the night sky, the crackling fire, and the particular voices of these two instruments that cried out to be combined. I didn't know much about ritual then; I was just making it up as I went along.

The bullroarer fascinated me. It's one of the most ancient instruments on the planet, basically a slotted piece of wood with a rope attached that is swung around the head in an arc emitting a sound that ranges – depending on the length of the rope and the shape of the wood – from a slow *whoooo* to a piercing shriek. Swing one over your head for ten or fifteen minutes and a globe of sound will form with you as the vortex. Whenever I did this I caught glimpses of animals and sometimes lost track of time altogether.

THE BULLROARER
*is one of the most
ancient instruments on
the planet.*

All this ended around the time of the *damaru*. Perhaps you've snapped awake in the middle of the night and found yourself sitting in the bed with your body on full alert, all the senses humming, but with nothing — no dream, no stranger rustling at the door — to account for your energized state. What I experienced was a little like that. Suddenly I snapped to attention, though there was nothing immediately apparent to account for my excitement, aside from my growing realization that I had been like a little kid playing with his father's tools, but playtime was over now; the work was about to begin. But what work?

One thing I can definitely date from the moment of that first *Binnngggg . . . Gunnngggg* is my awareness that I was living on a planet that was alive with odd and powerful instruments, many of them in my tradition as a percussionist. And though it was certainly true that no one I knew seemed interested in these instruments, particularly in their powers, that was no longer an excuse for me. It would be overstating things to say that what I felt was like a command; it was more like a hunger to collect and investigate as many of these instruments as I could find, as quickly as possible. Whenever I brought a new one into the Barn I tried to live with it for a while before playing it, making it welcome, quietly observing it. I didn't want any more unpleasant surprises.

This was mostly a private pursuit, though now that I had rejoined the band on stage, some of my experiments occasionally crossed over into my public life as a percussionist. I brought the *balafon* (an African marimba), the talking drum, and steel drums from the Caribbean on stage. I also played gongs, experimenting with all sorts of mallets, and grew very fond of the sound made when a hard rubber ball attached to the end of a chopstick was rubbed across the metal surface of the gong, creating a sound like the song of a humpbacked whale.

The two instruments that turned up most often in my onstage performances were the Beast and the Beam. The Beast — at least in its original form — was a circular stand on which I hung several large bass drums I played standing up, using large mallets. I still use a smaller version of this original conception in concert. The largest of the drums, which I call "home plate," produces the lowest drum sound I can make.

The Beam is an expansion on the idea that underlies the Pythagorean monochord; it illustrates the ancient perception that the divine was contained in certain mathematical relationships that could be turned into sound — the music of the cosmos. My first Beam was made out of driftwood, but almost from the beginning it was an instrument that mutated, assuming numerous forms until it achieved its current manifestation as a ten-foot aluminum girder. Stretching the entire length of the girder are twelve piano strings tuned to very low pitches (30 Hz) in pure unisons, octaves, and fifths. The vibrations are picked up by a magnetic pickup that's a giant version of the one you find on an electric guitar, except this one is fed into a 170,000-watt sound system.

The result is one of the most powerfully ethereal instruments I have ever played. The Beam can be an instrument of war or an instrument of peace. It can purr like a Tibetan choir or it can explode like napalm. I pluck it with my fingers or strike it with a metal pipe. Sometimes I kick it with the heel of my foot. You can get rough with the Beam without hurting its feelings – and it can get rough with you. You can go lower and deeper with the Beam than with anything else I know, descending into vibrations that are perceived less by the ear than felt as shockwaves throughout the body. There is nothing like a long vibrating string.

I usually play these instruments during the Rhythm Devils solo, when the other members of the band disappear, and Billy and I go exploring for fifteen or twenty minutes. The backbeat is one kind of drum groove; it's the essential one for rock and roll, but percussion can live in other grooves, and Kreutzmann and I have gradually evolved in those directions. All a groove is, really, is a rhythmic cycle that gets repeated over and over; it's a foundation you can build on. The stronger the groove, the higher the building you can erect, and the more elaborate the ornamentation. Temperamentally, I'm an ornamenter and Kreutzmann a foundation man, though we have played together enough that we frequently play against temperament.

We start on our drum sets, locking in the groove, and once we've sunk to a deep enough level one of us will usually head for the part of the stage where the Beast and Beam await. I think of it as the zone – once in the zone the point is to go somewhere you've never gone before. That's what we try for; it's what keeps us fresh. It's something the Grateful Dead has always tried to build into its music, but it's become increasingly harder to nurture the more successful we've become. The tension between our obligations to our audience and our obligations to the bond of exploration that first drew us together, between entertainment and art, is one that waxes and wanes but never disappears. Sometimes we dance the dance better than other times; sometimes we stumble: it's all part of the ride.

THE TWO
instruments that
turned up most often
in my onstage
performances were the
Beast (back) and the
Beam (front).
Ram Rod is at left.

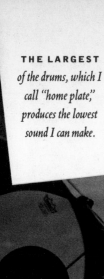

THE LARGEST *of the drums, which I call "home plate," produces the lowest sound I can make.*

HART, *Kreutzmann, and the Beast (above); the Rhythm Devils concert setup (right)*

Portrait of a Drummer at the Edge of Magic

187

THE BLIND
tar *maker sniffed
my tar and rubbed it
over his cheek,
caressing it like
a lover.*

IN THE LATE SEVENTIES THE BAND FELT THE NEED FOR SOMETHING magical. A proposal was made and accepted that we convince the Egyptian government to let us play at the Great Pyramids. Back in the sixties there were often moments of fantasy when we would imagine playing in the most incredible places – the Grateful Dead on the moon, the Grateful Dead at Versailles, the Grateful Dead at the Pyramids. To have one of these suddenly coming true lifted everyone's hearts. There was an upswell of anticipation throughout the Grateful Dead extended family, and in due course the trip became a family party whose cost would be partly defrayed by a live album deal. We would all go to Egypt to find a new groove.

The atmosphere in the streets of Cairo was electric the week we arrived, since Menachem Begin and Anwar Sadat had just begun the meetings at Camp David that would lead to the first Mideast peace accord. No one quite knew what to make of us. We played three nights. By the second night, Bedouins were riding in out of the desert to listen. You could see them from the stage, outlined against the dark horizon, silently observing us. On the third and last night they staked their camels, descended, and danced in their robes in front of the Sphinx.

Our opening act was a *tar* orchestra led by the great Nubian drummer Hamza el Din. I had met Hamza a few years earlier, when he suddenly showed up at the Barn, sent by Zakir and carrying his *tar*. We had tea and then Hamza played, and as soon as he did I realized that Zakir had sent me a master. Hamza had a way of teasing your mind with his rhythms. Just when you thought he was going one place, he'd fool you and smoothly accelerate into a different groove, the offbeat becoming the onbeat. He played with the One in a wonderful way, and the overall effect was a gentle flowing, a rhythmic lulling.

As soon as Hamza left, I began collecting *tars*. For years I was never without one. Wherever I went – parties, airplanes – my *tar* went. Having one close at hand steadied me. After a show, I used to sit in my hotel room for hours, recentering myself with the soft, pattering dance of its voice. The *tar's* quiet voice led me toward silence.

When the band's concerts at the Great Pyramids were over, I accompanied Hamza to his village, where John Cutler, my sound engineer, and I were hoping to record a traditional village *tar* orchestra. It was to be my first serious field recording, my first real foray with my Nagra to the Edge, which in Hamza's case was a collection of thatched-roof mud structures set for no apparent reason between this dune and that one, six hundred kilometers southwest of Cairo, right in the middle of the Nubian desert. At one time Hamza's people had been fishermen, but they had lost their village to modernity when the Aswan dam flooded their valley. And they had lost their traditional means of livelihood when the Egyptian government had relocated them to the edge of the desert.

When we arrived, the sun was blasting down onto the black ribbon of the road. In the distance castles shimmered up out of a blue-white ocean. Hamza's mother, a village elder, had died a few months earlier and this was the first chance Hamza had had to return and pay his respects, so he left us at his brother's house, then disappeared with him to visit his mother's grave. Before leaving he said to me, "You must surrender to the desert, Mickey."

Hours passed. The heat was unbearable. No one spoke English. John Cutler and I sat there staring at each other, brushing away the flies. Hamza's family brought us water and dates, and all the kids in the village strolled by to check out the strange white men. Finally I couldn't stand it any longer. I went outside with my *tar* and began to play a traditional festive groove, a wedding song.

The first time I'd ever met Hamza, at the Barn, he'd told me that the *tar* would sound different in the desert, and it did, startlingly richer and louder than I had ever heard it before. Suddenly, the street was full of *tars*. People were coming out of their houses with drums. Within ten minutes there must have been three dozen of us, singing and clapping and playing the *tar*. The women were all wearing beads and they made a nice rattling *sssshhhhhhhh* as they swayed and danced.

We sang for a long long time. Then Hamza returned, walking down the street with his brother, and our little festival came to a natural conclusion as everyone greeted Hamza and introductions were made all around. Later Hamza told me that there had been no music in the village since his mother's death, and that my playing the *tar* in public had been interpreted as the sign that the customary period of silent mourning for the passing of an elder was over.

OUR OPENING
act was a tar *orchestra*
led by the great
Nubian drummer
Hamza el Din.

*Portrait of
a Drummer
at the Edge
of Magic*
191

Among the introductions Hamza made was one to a blind *tar* maker who sniffed my *tar* and rubbed it over his cheek. He caressed it like a lover, felt it with the palms of his hands, cuddled it. There isn't a lot of wood in the Sahara – *tar* makers have to make do with whatever weathered scraps they can find – so my *tar,* finely crafted by a Sufi in Northern California, must have seemed like a Stradivarius. After thoroughly exploring it, the blind *tar* maker handed it back to me and indicated I should play something. I tapped the goatskin, and he was startled at the clarity of the sound and remarked about how balanced it was in its high and low frequencies; the maker of this drum was surely a master! Then I gave the *tar* to him and, holding it tenderly up to his ear, he began exciting the membrane and within seconds – *phhhhhhttt* – the drum trance.

The blind *tar* maker stood there and flowed with my *tar* for ten or fifteen minutes. Then he returned to the present time, smiled at Hamza and me, and handed the *tar* back with gracious thanks. It was as if he'd taken it out for a ride.

After dinner someone started a bonfire out in the desert, just a few dozen yards beyond the boundary of the village. All the *tar* players gathered into a big circle, and a single *tar* was passed around, each recipient singing a little verse that was quickly followed by a chorus from everyone present. In accordance with polite custom, a hash pipe was also making its way around the circle.

When it came my turn to sing, I just sang to them who I was, where I came from, and how wonderful it was to be with them. They couldn't understand what I was saying, and I couldn't understand what they were saying, as they chanted their response to each of my lines. But we kept this up until dawn.

At one point I lay back on the sand and stared up at the celestial lights. I was aware of so many things – of the existence of the drum brotherhood, of the way an instrument, particularly one with a strong dose of the spirit side, reflects the ecology of its birth, and perhaps most of all I was aware that I was lying on the outer edge of a vast continent that stretched away across the sands beyond my bare feet to the south and the west – Africa!

The drum continent. The Counterplayers.

CHAPTER TWELVE

Africa: The Invisible Counterplayers

HAVE BEEN MESMERIZED by Africa ever since I first heard my grandfather's stories. When I was a kid it excited me to think that there was a land where everyone drummed and danced, where you were surrounded by rhythm.

Those drums, those drums, my God, why don't they stop?

I realize now that I had absorbed the standard view of the "dark continent," with its fantastic, loud, orgiastic rituals in which the drum — scorned by European melodic music — was the dominant driver. Except that for me this wasn't a dangerous or negative image, but one that provoked a great yearning.

The German scholar and explorer Leo Frobenius, who led a number of expeditions to Africa in the early decades of this century, called the African cultures he observed "the invisible Counterplayers." *Invisible* because, lacking writing, they had no written history of their own and thus were granted no role in the histories of those who did; *Counterplayers* because Frobenius suspected that, although these cultures were unmentioned in the chronicles of antiquity, "I have no doubt that they worked upon the higher cultures, from the south."

The invisible Counterplayers – I liked that image.

Three hundred years ago Europe discovered these Counterplayers and began devouring them – killing, conquering, converting, enslaving, colonizing, modernizing, dispersing, in an eyeblink ravaging the ancient and beautiful civilizations of Africa, leaving only pale imitations of European cultures behind. Alan Lomax, a prominent Ethno, calls this disappearance "cultural greyout," and he predicts that in another generation nothing will be left of the Counterplayers but their artifacts, cleaned and carefully preserved and packed into tall metal cabinets in the catacombs of places like the Smithsonian.

All those drums – that's what I think of when I think of Africa's fate. Because, more so than those belonging to other areas, the tall metal containers assigned to Africa will be filled with drums. Drums with beautiful names: *ngoma, murumba, kalengo, babba ganga, atumpan, duono, embutu, mujaguzo.* Drums of all sizes and shapes. Log drums ten feet long and calabash drums that fit in your hand. Drums with elephantear membranes and drums that imitate the snarl of a leopard or the cry of a bird.

Frobenius felt that the Yoruba of West Africa were the most spiritual people in the world. I don't know about that, but I think it's to safe to say that Africans, particularly West Africans, are probably the most rhythmical, in the sense that an awareness and appreciation of rhythm is the mainstay of their culture. In most of Africa the proper rhythm and the proper life go hand in hand: a good person is one who is filled with the right rhythm. To be rhythmically attuned – to the cycles of nature, your own body, your fellow tribespeople – is one of the African Counterplayer's highest ideals, and it cannot be separated from the drum.

Of course, we're often reminded that the drum isn't the only musical instrument in black Africa, and it's not necessarily the most prominent. "All is not drumming in Africa south of the Sahara," writes a recent scholar, "though there are still many people in Europe who believe the contrary. Black Africa has a variety of stringed instruments, some of which rank among the most complex

"A VILLAGE *without music is a dead place," says an African proverb. There is a rhythm for every occasion that could ever require a rhythm.*

and melodious found in any culture." For instance, there's the twenty-one-string Mandinka instrument known as a *kora,* which can produce melodies of wonderful complexity and beauty. And then there's the three-man xylophone of the Baganda people of Uganda, the *akadinda;* a skilled *akadinda* trio can play approximately twelve notes a second.

But why diminish the importance of the drum and the complex rhythmic world it gives voice to? Why not just say that musically Africa represents an alternative evolution to that of the West, a musical culture whose emotional strategies may be different from but no less successful than European art music?

In much of Africa, music is as large a part of everyday life as conversation or cooking or the birdsong. It enhances the significance of all the important way stations of life, from birth through initiations to death. You can hear it in the marketplace, in the fields, and at night when the moon shines and when it doesn't shine. There are special songs sung when a child's first teeth erupt and songs sung to cure the same child of bed-wetting. There are songs sung when you're rowing a canoe and different ones for walking or hoeing in the fields — songs that are sung at these times and no other. You could almost say that African peoples have a song or a dance for every occasion. "A village without music is a dead place," says an African proverb.

Specifically you might say that there is a rhythm for every occasion that could ever require a rhythm. When the Minianka farmers of West Africa work in the fields with the short-handled hoe they call a *daba,* the drummers who accompany them play a rhythm perfectly suited to the *daba*'s motion. And there are special rhythms that help you sow seeds or worship the spirits. Inevitably some of these rhythms acquire words and become songs, and these songs stimulate certain body movements, becoming dances. The physical movements of the dancers are as much a part of the rhythmic cycle as the beat of the drum and the call and response of the voice.

THE FIRST ETHNOMUSICOLOGIST TO STUDY AFRICAN MUSIC SERIOUSLY was Erich von Hornbostel who in 1928 published an article that established three basic criteria to distinguish African music: antiphonal singing (call and response), polyphony (having two or more voices or parts, each with an independent melody but all harmonizing), and a highly developed rhythmic structure. African rhythm, he wrote, was "syncopated past comprehension."

The first time the Western ear listens to African music the result is often disorientation. Taught to expect a simple linear rhythm consisting of four beats to a measure, with the first and third accented, the Western classical musician finds it difficult to handle what ethnomusicologist John Chernoff calls "the dynamic clash and interplay of cross rhythms." African music is polyrhythmic. It is not uncommon to have three or four different rhythms occurring at any one time, which may strike our ears as hopelessly chaotic. The Western brain tries to entrain with this rhythmic chaos and pick out a dominant rhythm but, finding none, gives up, agreeing with Hornbostel that this music is beyond comprehension.

For a long time Western scholars were puzzled by how African musicians maintained any sense of time within this profusion of rhythmic patterns. Finally, ethnomusicologist Richard Waterman proposed that instead of trying to entrain with any one beat, Africans created a subjective rhythm within themselves — what a Fanti drum master calls the "hidden rhythm" — which they then bonded with all the other rhythms. The best way to keep time in a polyrhythm is to create a rhythm of your own and merge it with the group's. Apparently most Africans, both listeners and players, learn this truth at their parent's knee. When he studied the Venda of South Africa, John Blacking noted that whenever a little kid began banging some object, an adult or older child would instantly add a counterrhythm, transforming the child's spontaneous gesture into polyrhythmic play.

In *African Rhythm and African Sensibility,* the best discussion I found on these matters, John Chernoff, who has studied with a West African master drummer, reports that a beginning African musician concentrates all his energy on listening to his own rhythm, and only his own rhythm. Eventually, as he becomes more proficient, the student reaches a point where the drum is said to beat itself. Only then is he allowed to listen to the rest of the music. And only then is he considered a drummer. Chernoff's own drum teacher told him that only when he was able to listen to two rhythms at once and not lose his place would he be a true African drummer.

Chernoff explains that when he was just learning to drum, he was given a ritually prepared bundle of drumsticks that had once belonged to the great master drummers of the tribe, and he was told to put them under his pillow. I nearly dropped the book when I read this, because I used to do the same thing with Lenny's sticks. When I was nine or ten, I used to put the snakewood sticks under my pillow and hope that I would absorb my father's drumming power. Later, when I began playing with the Grateful Dead, I would sometimes take sticks that had lasted a whole set – particularly if the set had been a fiery one, one that had summoned the big groove – and I'd put them under my pillow for strength.

Chernoff makes it clear that Africans do not improvise, at least not in the way we think of improvisation in the West. Most of the rhythms and songs are traditional, allowing very little latitude for individual experimentation. The ideal, here as elsewhere in African culture, is to fit one's own personal rhythms seamlessly into the flow of the whole. You might call this rhythm sharing. Musically the rhythm of each drum in an ensemble is comparatively simple, consisting of endless variations on duple and triple time. It's only when these rhythms are combined that the complexity becomes impressive, threes beating against fours, throbbing and pulsing, creating a kind of bodily tension in listeners that is best released by dancing.

Most of the drums in an ensemble will be engaged in purely rhythmic cycles, laying down the beat for the dancers. But there is usually one drummer, the master drummer, who will be drumming coded signals that tell the musicians and dancers when to start and stop various patterns, and woven throughout will be the commentary of the master drummer.

The master drummer of a West African ensemble is like the senior percussionist in a Western orchestra. His position depends as much on mastery of drum lore as on technical skill; in Africa it's hard to separate the two. Knowing the right rhythm to play on an occasion is as important as being able to execute that rhythm. When the chief gets up from his stool and begins strolling, the master drummer must be able to switch rhythms effortlessly. He might, to borrow an example from ethnomusicologist J. H. Kwabena Nketia, play a rhythm that repeats the message: "The chief walks. He is not in a hurry." Besides calling attention to the fact that the chief is up and moving, this little rhythm also impresses upon the chief that he should walk carefully and consciously; stumbling would be a bad omen.

Master drummers are full of this sort of stuff. A good master drummer at a social dance can keep up a regular monologue on his drum, telling jokes and proverbs, rapping out rhythms that might say "hi" to specific people in the audience or call others up to dance. We call this the "talking"

THE CLASSIC
*variable-pitch talking
drum, the* dundun

drum, and for centuries it was one of the most mysterious things about the drum continent. Chernoff tells a story of how he was sitting one afternoon with a drum master, learning some basic rhythms, when suddenly the man deviated from the rhythm he was playing, just for a few seconds, then returned to the lesson. A few minutes later a man who had been walking by at the time returned with two beers. That little rhythmic deviation had actually been the equivalent of a shouted, "Hey, friend, get us a couple of cold ones." The Gahu, an Ewe social dance, begins with the drums beating out the message, "All you girls with big bottoms come out and start shaking."

The classic variable-pitch talking drum, the *dundun,* is an hourglass-shaped, two-headed drum, its heads laced together by gut strings or thongs of leather. The *dundun* is held under the arm and played with one hand. By squeezing the strings with the other hand, the player is able to change the tension of the head, thus altering the pitch of the sounds he is making.

Basically Africans get their drums to talk by creating multiple tones or rhythms – combinations of high and low, long and short. Some African languages are tonal, so relative pitch affects meaning: a sound rising means one thing; the exact same sound dropping off means something quite different. In nontonal languages, rhythmic patterns can symbolically represent these differences. By creating drums capable of handling pitch at the same time as rhythm, the Africans figured out a way to turn rhythm and noise into speech. Today, the old societies that preserved the languages of the drum are almost completely wiped out, overrun by telephones, cars, and TV, all of which convey information more quickly and perhaps with greater accuracy.

At the high end of the African talking drum phenomenon is the "bush telegraph." During their library research run, the Ethnos turned up dozens of stories like the following from an English missionary: "In 1881 we in Landana heard of the wreck of the mail steamer *Ethiopia* off Luango, 60 or 70 miles away, one or two hours after its actual occurrence in Luango, by drum message. This wonderful drum is called *nkonko,* and is formed of a log of wood some six feet long. . . . A good operator with his drumsticks can say anything he likes upon it in his dialect. The drum-language (so called) is not limited to a few sentences, but, given a good operator and a good listener, comprehends all that a man can say."

This was the famous bush telegraph, and it looked like sophisticated technology in a place where there wasn't supposed to be any sophisticated technology. It took years for us to accept the fact that these big slit gongs,

THE FAMOUS
bush telegraph

ingeniously positioned to utilize the acoustical properties of the rivers and valleys, were in effect a relay system of giant bullhorns that produced tones that were audial copies of actual words.

The bush telegraph was first seriously studied in the thirties by J. F. Carrington, who observed its use in what is now Zaire. Carrington discovered that, although sophisticated, there were some practical limitations to the circulation of news using slit gongs. First, you had the carrying limits of the gongs: about five miles by day and, at most, seven by night. To send a message twenty miles required four separate transmissions, and that's where the efficiency of the system broke down. Second, Africa is a veritable Tower of Babel; the place has over a thousand languages, and untold more dialects, so messages that cover any distance have to pass through numerous translations, which means an efficient bush telegraph must have on hand a couple of linguists and a couple of drummers working in tandem. In boundary towns like Yakusu, wrote Carrington, it was possible "to hear drums beating in four quite different drum languages any day."

IF THE TRIBES OF CENTRAL ASIA ARE THE CLASSIC EXAMPLE OF A shamanic trance culture, then those of Africa are their counterpart among possession trance cultures. Instead of the shaman riding his drumbeat to the World Tree where he meets with the spirit world, Africans, particularly West Africans, believe that the spirits ride the drumbeat down into the body of the dancers, who then begin the erratic shaking movements of the possessed.

Possession trance is the opposite of shamanic trance in almost every way. The shaman frequently remains conscious throughout the shamanic trance state, even going so far as to share with his audience the various conversations that are taking place in the spirit world. If called upon, he can give a blow-by-blow account of what he is experiencing. During a possession trance, the possessed's consciousness is said to leave and go wandering while the spirit is in residence. Where this consciousness goes and what happens while the spirit is occupying its place are completely unknown to those who have been possessed. Typically they have no memory of anything that has happened and couldn't begin to tell you what the possessing spirit says through them. Nor, curiously, can many of the onlookers, since only a few initiates acquire the ability to interpret the secret language the spirits speak.

In most African possession cults the spirits that do the possessing are actually those of ancestors. According to John Blacking, who witnessed possession among the Venda, the possessed person "attained a somatic state in which he or she became more than usually conscious of the life-force in the body," a condition that brought the person "face to face with his or her other self, the real self of the ancestor spirit." This is not an unusual or mysterious state for the Venda, "a gift of grace for a chosen few," but is available to all who learn how to use their bodies correctly.

In West Africa, where there is a rich literature on possession, these potent ancestor spirits are called *Orisha,* which literally means "he whom Ori (the head) has picked out for distinction." The Yoruba say that anyone who does something so great that it can never be forgotten becomes an *Orisha.* And some become so famous that their status begins to approach the godlike.

Shango, who is worshiped all over West Africa, South America, and the Caribbean as the *Orisha* of thunder and lightning, was originally a powerful warrior who, though generous and noble, was also quick-tempered, tyrannical, and an eventual suicide. Shango knew much magic, including the secret of thunder.

Shango, Kori (the goddess of fertility), and Ogun (the god of iron and war) are all examples of *Orisha* who have inspired their own cults and are worshiped by thousands of people. But there are also humble *Orisha* of the hearth, who might be a grandfather or a great-grandmother, someone whose life was so meaningful that the succeeding generations have deemed it prudent to keep the door open in order to enjoy their wise counsel. It's as if we had a technology that would allow us to keep in contact with Pythagoras or Gandhi or Krupa.

To understand how this is possible it helps to know how the West Africans view the psyche. For them, the head – Ori – contains not only the personal consciousness but is also the abode of the creator spirit, though their description of this abode suggests that it's a doorway. The ego can go out the door, leaving the room open for the *Orisha* to enter through the head and then take over the whole body. Yayo Diallo, who is a Minianka and the author of an excellent memoir, *The Healing Drum,* writes that "in a state of trance the individual loses normal self-awareness. The Minianka say that a spirit has mounted the individual's body and displaced the person's double." Diallo tells of seeing a man in trance leap into a well and then right out again "as if propelled by springs. He was not just playing around with an abundance of energy; something beyond him was playing with his body."

NOT ALL POSSESSING SPIRITS ARE *ORISHA,* AND YOU DON'T WANT TO be possessed by just any spirit, so great care must be taken that only the correct spirit takes up residence. The way this is accomplished is with the drum. Particular rhythms are supposed to attract particular spirits. An *Orisha* like Shango only comes when he hears his rhythm.

The most powerful trance rhythms belong to secret societies, which handle all communication between this world and the spirit world. The Yewe secret society of West Africa has seven different types of drum rhythm that accompany the sect's seven special dances and attract seven different spirits.

Societies like the Yewe are very secretive. New members move into one of the sect's initiation houses and remain isolated there for many months, learning the sect's language, its rhythms, dances, and powers. In some sense they resemble the shaman schools, except their classes are much, much larger. Although in some tribes every young person is initiated into one secret society or another, the best candidates are often those who are undergoing some sort of traumatic psychic episode – they might be found one morning lying unconscious or wandering dazed in the bush. Their experience is interpreted as offering an opening to the spirit world, and the sufferer is quickly taken up and initiated.

Not much has been written about what goes on during these initiation rites, but bits and pieces can be found in the literature, particularly in studies of some of the New World appearances of the possession sects, like candomblé, vôdun, and santería. Some of these sects seem to have discovered ways to keep their young initiates in trance for months. In general two types of trance are seen. One is the full-blown possession trance, where the spirit is actually in residence. What's more common is a kind of light trance that in candomblé is often accompanied by a regression to infantile states. It is said that the god, having departed, leaves a young child to keep its place.

During the training for their initiation, candidates are taught the drum rhythms that will summon the sect's spirits, as well as the assorted secret languages and cues that will be used. What happens can be explained by what contemporary psychology calls "state dependent learning." According to this theory, when the body experiences stress it encodes certain cues that will be regenerated the next time the body finds itself in a similar situation. The body of an initiate is methodically stressed to the point of trance, and the application of this stress is accompanied by certain overt cues in the form of drum rhythms and dance movements. Apparently the brain begins to associate these cues with the desired trance state, until it is necessary only to play these rhythms and your body begins to respond involuntarily. So the drum rhythms act not only as a signal to a particular spirit, but also as cues that trigger the learned trance response among the dancers.

ONE OF THE MOST INTERESTING PAPERS ON AFRICA THAT CAME MY way was by an academic named Daniel F. McCall, a synopsis of an unfinished book that he had been working on for decades tentatively entitled *West Africa and the Eurasian Ecumene*. McCall had called his extract "Mother Earth: The Great Goddess of West Africa."

According to McCall, eight or nine thousand years B.C., Neolithic culture, with its worship of the Great Mother, stretched from Central Europe to the then fertile grasslands of the Sahara. As the Sahara turned to desert, the cultures living in it retreated, some moving south and west into the region we now know as West Africa. As the desert advanced, these cultures were pushed deeper into the forest, which then closed around them providing a shield that preserved the old Neolithic goddess cultures for thousands of years more. Mounted invaders didn't reach the forest until sometime between A.D. 500 and 1000.

McCall's thesis that the West African possession trance cultures were actually a remnant of the Neolithic mother goddess tradition reminded me of something I had read in Gilbert Rouget's *Music and Trance*. In his chapter on the ancient Greeks, Rouget had gone to great lengths to prove that many of the ecstatic religions that had so annoyed Greek rationalists like Plato were in fact possession cults. The Greeks had known four different kinds of trance: erotic trance, poetic trance, mantic trance, and something Socrates called telestic trance. According to Rouget, this last trance, which comes from the Greek teletai, meaning "ritual," was a possession trance. Amidst frenzied dancing, which Plato in the *Republic* banned as "unfit for our citizens," the spirits of the cult came down and took up residence in the bodies of the dancers.

What Rouget had not bothered to explore was the interesting fact that all these possession cults — the Corybantes, the Bacchantes, the cult of Cybele, the Dionysian cults — were all surviving fragments of the ancient goddess religions, all of them trance possession cultures in which drums were probably the driving mechanism. At one point in the play *The Bacchae*, Dionysius cries out, "O my sisterhood of worshipers, whom I lead with me from barbaric countries, Timolus, bastion of Lydia, who live and travel at my side. Raise the music of your own country, the Phrygian drums invented by Rhea the Great Mother, and by me."

One day I picked up a classical music dictionary and looked up the few percussion instruments known to the ancient world. Almost all of them were mentioned in connection with the surviving cults of the Great Mother:

> *Krotala:* A percussion instrument consisting of two hollow pieces of shell, wood, or metal in various forms; clappers. The *krotala* were used, like the castanets, to keep the rhythm of the dancers, especially in honor of Cybele and Dionysius. They were usually fastened one on each hand.

> *Tympanum:* Percussion instrument in use especially in the rites of Cybele and Dionysius. It was made of a cylindrical box with skin membranes stretched on both sides; it was played by the hand, usually by women.

> *Roptron:* A tambourine in the modern sense, i.e., a small and light drum consisting of a wooden hoop with a piece of parchment over it, and small pieces of metal fastened around it. It was used by the Corybantes (priests of Cybele) in their ceremonies.

Was there, immediately preceding Western "history," a drum-driven possession trance culture that worshiped the earth in the form of a Great Mother? Suddenly a lot of things clicked into place. I remembered those

pictures in Marija Gimbutas's book of what seemed to be African-looking drums that had been excavated in places like Bulgaria and Germany from around 4500 B.C. and that were no longer around a thousand years later, when the first modern cities appeared in the Tigris-Euphrates watershed.

I remembered Gimbutas writing that there was "an intimate relation between the drum and the goddess." I remembered the puzzlement I'd felt as I watched the drum dwindle in importance as a Western musical instrument, at one point almost disappearing, even from the military. Was this near extinction due to the fact that the drum had been part of a possession trance culture that had been suppressed by its conquerors (the notorious Indo-Europeans), who came in successive waves out of the Central Asian steppes and who worshiped the male sky gods we find in place as written history begins?

Was the drum a casualty of this collision? Certainly the Neolithic religion of the goddess was. It literally disappears from our history, is all but wiped out, except for the bit of it — if McCall is correct — that withdraws into the West African forest, nurturing a culture that Leo Frobenius will one day call the most spiritual in the world.

THE INVISIBLE COUNTERPLAYERS.

Three hundred years ago Europe began devouring them, beginning the long journey to the metal cabinets, an image that haunts me and I would find alarmingly depressing if I didn't also realize that it's never that simple. Even diluted and dismembered, cultures can retain potency, indeed can mutate in the most startling ways.

For example: when the slave ships began plying the waters between the New World and West Africa, everyone thought they carried just strong, expendable bodies. But they were also carrying the Counterplayer culture — maybe even the mother goddess culture — preserved in the form of drum rhythms that could call down the *Orisha* from their time to ours. In the Caribbean and South America, slaves were allowed to keep their drums and thus preserved their vital connection with the *Orisha*, though the sudden mingling of so many different tribes produced new variations like candomblé,

THE CORYBANTES, *the Bacchantes, the cult of Cybele, the Dionysian cults — these were all surviving fragments of the ancient goddess religions.*

santería, and vôdun. But in North America the slaves were not allowed to keep their drums and they lost the means by which to keep the rhythms of their spirit world alive.

And out of this severing came jazz, the blues, the backbeat, rhythm and blues, rock and roll – some of the most powerful rhythms on the planet.

CHAPTER THIRTEEN

THE BROTHERHOOD OF THE DRUM

HERE IS A NEED TO DRUM. I believe that. No drummer really knows why, you're just born with it, it's what makes you part of Remo Belli's one percent. You can acquire technique but not this need, it's a birthright. There have been times when I wished I'd been born without it. When I was younger, if I didn't play well, I'd feel like killing myself. I used to slip on stage before a show and pray — pray that I didn't screw up, that my energy and talent and will would be strong enough to carry me to the Edge one more time.

211

I often wonder what kind of drummer I might have become if I had been born into a culture with a tradition of the spirit side of the drum, instead of one with no road maps, no way of talking about those energies and powers you encounter when you play. I often regret that I never spoke of this with Sonny Payne or Jonesy or any of the other older men who should have been my teachers in this matter, if only they'd had something to teach. Did they know about the spirit side? Did they care? Did they feel any pain that we were born into a culture where music was entertainment first, a commodity of the marketplace, and you either accommodated to that or found another way of living?

I remember as a kid being afraid of what was going to happen to me. The image of the musician as a kind of human meteorite who blazed briefly across the sky before burning up was strong during my childhood. Charlie Parker and Billie Holiday — these were heroes and warnings. I used to wonder what it was about this need that had chosen me that it could make a grown man give up everything, even to the point of relinquishing life, to achieve what was usually the briefest of connections. Sometimes I felt that I was running as fast as I could with a blindfold on.

It is hard to pinpoint the exact moment when I awoke to the fact that my tradition — rock and roll — did have a spirit side, that there was a branch of the family that had maintained the ancient connection between the drum and the gods. I suppose it was a little like meeting some long lost cousins and realizing with a start that these are your relatives, that you are rhythmically related, and in drumming that's the same as blood.

I remember picking up a newspaper one day and seeing that Babatunde Olatunji and his "Drums of Passion" were playing at a local club in the Bay Area. I couldn't believe it! I had completely forgotten about Olatunji. He'd become a record that I'd worn out when I was eighteen, a faded snapshot of those sleek cosmopolitan bodies at Raphael Baez's parties in Spain, pulsating to the big West African polyrhythms.

When I got to the club, I discovered that my Grateful Dead stage manager was running the mixing board. He graciously allowed me to take over. I counted the drums on the stage — sixteen. I'd never seen that many on one small stage before. It reminded me of Diga, a big rhythm machine of tuned percussion.

Olatunji appeared wearing white robes and a beautiful hat. Tall and regal, he looked more like an elder statesman than a musician, an impression that was strengthened as soon as his ensemble began playing. I cranked the PA system up as loud as it would go and leaned back to watch. Within minutes he and his group established a deep groove of enormous power. I could see the

OLATUNJI
*appeared wearing
white robes and a
beautiful hat. Tall and
regal, he looked
more like an elder
statesman than
a musician.*

veins on their foreheads popping out with the force of their concentration. This was not entertainment. This wasn't a stage show. This was serious, this was some sort of invocation. But to what?

OLATUNJI'S TALE

Where I come from we say that rhythm is the soul of life because the whole universe revolves around rhythm, and when we get out of rhythm, that's when we get into trouble. For this reason the drum, next to the human voice, is our most important instrument. It is special.

For many years I have thought about the healing power of the drum, and the philosophy I have come to is that the drum is a kind of trinity. The body of the drum, which comes from a tree, contains the living spirit of that tree. Great care is taken to make sure that the wood of the drum is alive. And the same is true of the skin; whether it is the tanned hide of a goat or a buffalo, it also contains a spirit that is still alive. And when you join these two spirits with that of the person playing the drum, the result is an irresistible force, a trinity, a balance that gives the drum its healing power.

I was born in West Africa, in Yoruba land, in a place where there were five or six villages, each a couple of miles apart. Every weekend there would be dancing and music in one village or another, and even as a little boy I would walk over and watch – the drummers in particular. Sometimes the master drummers would let me carry their drums, and in return they'd give me a lesson.

There was no school for drumming. It's like in the United States where there's a playground on every corner, and the little boys and girls play basketball or baseball. In my village there was always music and everyone would grab something to play. Those of us who became drummers were simply the ones who went beyond that common exposure and learned the craft.

My first instrument was a cowbell. The first rhythm I learned was what we call *conconcolo,* which is a very simple rhythm but difficult to hold. The first time you play with master drummers they will usually say, "Grab the bell and let's hear you play *conconcolo.*" Sometimes you have to hold the *conconcolo* beat for hours. The next time they let you play with them they will say, "Take the bell again," and only after many times like this will they let you play the shaker, and then finally the drum.

The first drum I had made for me was called *apesi*. The *apesi* is a clay drum, shaped like a hourglass, which is covered with woven cane for protection. My mother was a potter, so she made me my first one. With its woven cane covering, the *apesi* is a beautiful drum, but you only have to drop it once.

It takes years to become a master drummer. The reason for this is that you have to know not only the rhythms but the dances as well. As a drummer, you have to be able to dance; you have to know all the songs and all the dances that go with them. Once you know all the parts of all the dances, then you will be given the opportunity to lead the band. You become the heir apparent, the keeper of the rhythms.

Many of these rhythms are only played at specific times, during the festival for a house raising, for example. Or when a drought occurs, we have a rhythm for that, a dance that is done only at that time. But the most important rhythms in Yoruba land are those that communicate with the *Orisha*. There are many *Orisha,* so many that no one can name them all at once. The Yoruba say that anyone who does something so great that he or she can never be forgotten has become an *Orisha*. There are several ways of celebrating these *Orisha*. Sometimes we make sacrifices at the shrine of the *Orisha* and offer them gifts. Or else a feast with drumming and dancing is planned, and as we chant and dance, some of the people will become possessed by the spirit of, say, Ogun or Shango and be transformed to a higher spiritual level.

I never became a master drummer in the old sense of knowing all the village rhythms, because when I was twenty-three – in 1950 – I won a scholarship to college in Atlanta. I came by boat, arriving in New Orleans. I was going to study sociology. My drumming was behind me I thought; I'd only brought a small frame drum to amuse myself on board the ship.

But when I got to college and first turned on the radio and heard, "When I love my baby, every time it rains I think of you and I feel blue," I was so stunned. I remember thinking, hey that's African music; it sounds like what's at home. And the same thing happened when I heard gospel music. So I joined the campus jazz combo.

AIRTO

stalked the stage, a hungry animal foraging for sounds, ringing bells, blowing whistles, and occasionally emitting barking guttural chants, usually in Portuguese.

I FIRST MET THE GREAT SOUTH AMERICAN DRUMMER AIRTO MOREIRA while I was working on the score for Francis Coppola's *Apocalypse Now.* Anyone who has ever seen that movie knows that its centerpiece is the trip the character played by Martin Sheen makes up the river in search of the renegade warrior played by Marlon Brando. Francis had transposed Joseph Conrad's novel *Heart of Darkness* to the Vietnam War, and he wanted to create a soundscape that would accompany this river journey, gently drawing the filmgoer deeper and deeper into the surreal and dangerous world of the jungle. He wanted to create sounds nobody had ever heard before and tune them to a precise emotional pitch.

I love gathering sounds. For years it had been one of my deepest private passions; now Francis was pushing it public and I felt that rush of panic and excitement that is the adrenaline of art. The first thing I did was scatter monitors all over the Barn and screen *Apocalypse* constantly. For weeks it was going all day long, always in the background, just the footage and dialogue, until finally I began to dream about it, the movie entering my dreamtime; after that it was with me constantly.

As I assembled my soundscape it began to bother me that none of the percussionists I had in mind to play the score had ever been to the jungle. When it came to understanding the spirit of the place, we were tourists. It was then I thought of Airto.

Airto was South American, a Brazilian. I'd first seen him years before with Miles Davis. He had played like a man possessed, so intense and serious that he made Miles, who isn't exactly passive, look like a man out for an afternoon stroll. Airto stalked the stage, a hungry animal foraging for sounds, ringing bells, blowing whistles, and occasionally emitting barking guttural chants, usually in Portuguese.

I was expecting the jungle from Airto. What I got was a mirror image of myself. He arrived with a working kit of his own devising, lots of whistles and strange little buzzing devices — small, discrete sounds that were the opposite of the big, loud, overpowering noises that I favored. It was characteristic of Airto that he had always known what had taken me years to learn: that if

a drummer needed a special sound he either makes it himself or goes without. Airto even had a pair of wooden shoes from Holland that he'd clap together whenever he needed a really solid *thunk*. Airto was into it like I was into it.

He lived with me for the three weeks it took to record *Apocalypse*. I was fascinated by him. He was so *there* as a drummer, so conscious of the rhythm, yet it was a completely natural attunement, not a highly educated one like Zakir's or Olatunji's. Airto had an ability to give himself to the act of playing and to the rhythmic possibilities that were always unfolding. He was magnetic to watch, and powerful, for me at least. He was dealing with a much darker palette than I was, exploring a different emotional family of sounds than the one I was familiar with.

I'd been collecting and playing drums long enough to know that this wasn't solely a function of Airto's temperament; the instruments played a big part. Airto's instruments — the wood block, the whistle, the bullroarer, the *berimbau* (or musical bow) were so much older than any of the instruments I'd ever played. Particularly the *berimbau,* a single vibrating string that runs down a long stick neck attached to an open gourd. The left hand balances the long neck of the bow, while the right hand, holding a stick and a rattle, strikes the string, producing a droning, throbbing buzz whose pitch can be changed by manipulating the open part of the gourd against your stomach.

We used to stand around the fireplace in the Barn, Airto playing the *berimbau,* I the *tar,* telling stories. I told him about the *damaru,* about the rudiments, and slowly, as the weeks passed, he told me who he was:

THE RHYTHMIST'S TALE

I was born in 1941 in a small village in southern Brazil. When I was only a few months old I began making erratic physical movements that alarmed my mother. Concerned that I might have some strange disease, my mother went to grandmother, and while they were discussing me I suddenly began twitching and rocking. "See," my mother said, "there, he's doing it now." My grandmother watched me intently and then she stood and crossed the room and turned off the radio. I immediately stopped rocking. I'm told my grandmother then turned to my mother and exclaimed, "Oh my God! We've got another musician in the family."

My grandmother's exclamation was not a completely happy one, though it was she who later gave me my first drum, a toy tambourine. You see, her husband, my mother's father, was an Italian immigrant from Milan, a crazy man, I'm told, a night person, a bohemian, a drinker, never at home much or at work much, though when he was he was a fine tailor. Only one thing consumed him – the opera. My grandfather lived for the concerts that he put on out of his own pocket. Whatever extra cash he had was spent on his art, not his family.

When I was a few years older I used to go to the dances on Sunday afternoons. I never danced, I always watched the drummers. Sometimes they would let me play a shaker or a tambourine. I got my first regular job as a percussionist when I was six, accompanying an old man who played button accordion. We would go by horse, sometimes five or six hours from my town, to play at big Polish or German weddings. The bride's family would host a big barbecue to feed the hundreds of guests. The cooks would roast a half dozen pigs, a couple of goats, and maybe a cow. We'd play five or six songs, get the people really in a groove, dancing like crazy, and then we'd stop and pass the hat.

When I say I played percussion I mean that I played the gourd rattles. At that time in Brazil a percussionist was called a rhythmist and was paid much less than an actual drummer.

I didn't play my first real drum, a drum set actually, until I was eight. That happened at *carnaval*. My mother, father, sister, and I had gone to a dance, but I was so young they didn't want to let me in. I began crying and finally they said okay, I could stay, but I would have to remain up on stage with the band. They thought I'd be safe up there. And the band's drummer didn't show up. He missed his bus or something. Now the band leader knew I was a rhythmist so he asked if I wanted to try the drums. I remember well, there was a big bass drum with a little cymbal on top on a spring, plus some coconuts and wooden blocks, and an old bicycle horn beside the traps. The band leader said, "Play a march," and I did. I played a march, then a samba, and that was the start of my career as a professional drummer, because when the night was over the band leader gave me forty new *pais* and then went and asked my father if I could come work with his band as their drummer.

I found the drum set very interesting. Instead of holding and playing and moving, I found myself sitting and beating with two things I

THE BERIMBAU
was used in the
slave's martial art,
capoeira.

held in my hands, the sticks, and I was amazed at the number of different rhythms I could get going. It struck me as very odd and I had to try hard not to listen to what I was playing, because whenever I did, the strangeness of it would make me forget what I was playing and I would get confused.

I do not mind playing a drum set but in some sense it is too rhythmic for my temperament. You have to sit there and play rhythm and you have to stick with it because if you stop there's a hole in the music. Percussion is more my style, colors and effects. If I had to choose I would play very little rhythm and lots of other stuff. I like to be on my feet and move when I play. For this reason my favorite drum early on was the *pandeiro,* the tambourine.

We did not have many hand drums in Brazil, just the *pandeiro* and the *atabaque,* which is a drum like a conga or a *bata,* straight and much bigger on top than on bottom. I didn't get in touch with the *atabaque* until I was almost twenty, when I was playing in the Quarteto Novo in São Paulo. Even now, though I play *atabaque,* I think of it mostly as a spirit instrument.

The *atabaque* and the *berimbau,* the bow — for me they represent the wonderful culture that was brought to Brazil by the black slaves of Angola. They brought us umbanda and candomblé and with these they taught us patience and how to be strong. How to take pain, without complaining, how to be patient with people who have no consideration for you, for other human beings. Insensitive people.

The *berimbau,* you know, was used in the slaves' martial art, *capoeira.* The slaves were not allowed to practice *capoeira* openly or it would have seemed to the plantation guards that they were practicing for war. So while they fought they played the *berimbau* in a particular rhythm and whenever anyone spotted a guard the rhythm would change and everyone would start dancing. The guard would come and look and say, "Oh, good. The slaves are happy. So let's leave 'em alone, let's get out of here." As soon as they were gone the rhythm of the *berimbau* would change and they'd start fighting or training again.

We play the *atabaque* in candomblé and umbanda, in the times when a medium is present. I myself belong to what in English would be called a chain. This is a group of people, friends and family members, neighbors, who get together to think the same thoughts. We sit in a circle and there are drummers playing certain rhythms. The *Orisha* – the spirits – come down into the body of the medium and you can talk to them. You might say, "Well, what should I do about this and what should I do about that," and usually they will give you advice. And they know all about you. You can't fool them. They might come back at you and say, "Well, what about this, what about that." And then everybody will know about this and that.

You can't leave your body too open during one of these sessions. Sometimes spirits will get into somebody beside the medium. If you're not keeping your mind clear on what is happening, if you're thinking about problems, then sometimes bad things can happen. Because the spirits are like us. Some are on a very high level of awareness and some are on a very low level. There are bad spirits and good spirits, just like us.

Shango is supposed to be my half father because he was the one who baptized me. I was baptized in the spirit by Shango, so I am a son of Shango. But there are thousands or millions of spirits who belong to the Shango level. Otherwise Shango couldn't be in Brazil and Cuba at the same time, so when we say Shango we mean all the spirits around the world who are on that level.

ONE NIGHT, TOWARD THE END OF THE *APOCALYPSE* SESSIONS, AIRTO gave me a *berimbau* and a magic rock to play it with. He knew I was attracted to the bow. Whenever he played it during the sessions, I would stop what I was doing to watch. That sound, that quiet humming vibrating buzzing sound, seemed to work directly on my nervous system. I could taste the jungle, I could smell it, it reeked of danger.

I became obsessed with the *berimbau*. For the third or fourth time in my musical life I found myself falling into a state in which I did nothing but practice a new instrument. It had happened last with the *tar*. I hardly slept for the next three or four weeks, rarely washed, barely ate, and was mostly uncommunicative, feeding on the strange rhythms of the bow, rhythms to which I seemed particularly susceptible – they tranced me out in minutes.

The bow got me interested in the percussive possibilities of gourds. Since decent gourds were expensive and difficult to obtain, the obvious solution was to grow them myself and make my own rattles and shakers. I made dozens of gourd shakers and *berimbaus*. Because the shakers from South America or Africa are usually covered with glass beads, I began asking around in the Bay Area for a glass bead maker and was eventually contacted by Michael Pluznick who, beside being a bead maker, was a drummer.

It took Pluznick months to make enough beads to cover one of my big shakers. Each time I saw him I noticed slight changes in his appearance. He began wearing white all the time, and he told me that he was playing the *bata*, the big two-headed cylinder drum that lies lengthways across your lap as you play it with both hands. Its origin is West Africa, where it's usually combined into a trio to form one of the classic drum ensembles – a mother, father, and baby drum – that are used to summon the *Orisha*.

Pluznick, it turned out, had become involved in santería, which is the name the West African possession trance religions had assumed in Cuba. Not only was he playing the *bata* in the rituals, he was also studying to be a santería priest and he invited me to his induction. It was held in San Francisco, in a community center. There were maybe a hundred and fifty people squeezed into a modest room. Everyone looked very clean, very clear-eyed, and healthy. There were a lot of kids running around, though as soon as the drums started everyone grew still. I couldn't believe how loud these drums were – they dominated the room, as did the chief drummer, a man named Francisco Aguabella. Aguabella was the dean of santería drummers in the Bay Area. He was an elderly man, maybe sixty-five years old, but his arms were some of the most powerful I have ever seen. When he hit the *bata* it was like a hammer hitting a nail.

I didn't know what spirits he was calling. I remember wondering if you could keep a spirit alive for hundreds, maybe even thousands of years if there are enough people to – to what? To say the name, sing the songs, play the music, preserve the rhythms? I remembered McCall's thesis that the West African drum-driven religions preserved elements of the old goddess religion of the Neolithic. If that was true, then these rhythms were some of the most resilient on the planet. Five, ten, twenty thousand years – who knows how long they have been pulsing?

IT WAS DIFFERENT IN THE UNITED STATES. HERE THE SLAVES WERE NOT allowed to keep their drums. The story is that slaveholders feared the drum's ability to talk and worried that in the event of a slave revolt the instruments might provide a means of communication. So they were banned or destroyed in most areas of the Republic with the exception of the parishes around New Orleans. There the drums were reportedly allowed and the polyrhythmic tradition lived on, accompanied by its possession dances, making New Orleans the only area in America where the *Orisha* established a strong foothold.

That's the general outline of the usual story. It's hazy because facts are hard to come by. We don't know for sure that the African slaves in these parishes were allowed to keep their drums, though there is some evidence that New Orleans, with its heavily French and Spanish influence, was one of the rare places where blacks were allowed to gather for their own entertainments, which included singing and dancing and presumably drumming. Nor is there any concrete evidence that an indigenous American brand of vôdun emerged in New Orleans, though by the time of the Revolution the practice of vôdun in these parts was sufficiently popular among the slaves to be considered a social danger. But judging from the early decrees, the infection was perceived to be coming from the Caribbean. By 1800 the governor of Louisiana had banned the buying of all blacks from Martinique, Haiti, and Santo Domingo, largely because of the cult of vôdun, but also because there was a perceived link between vôdun and the slave revolts that were rippling across the Caribbean. The 1791 revolt in Haiti was supposed to have begun at a vôdun ceremony.

But for some reason the governor later lifted the ban in 1803, and New Orleans was immediately flooded with refugees from Haiti and Santo Domingo, which led to an intensification of the vôdun cult. By 1817 the religion had progressed to the point that the New Orleans city council felt it necessary to ban all public meetings of blacks, except for those held in a designated field in the center of today's New Orleans, where every Sunday the slaves were allowed to gather for dancing. This field later became known as Congo Square.

Michael Ventura, in a wonderful essay on this subject entitled "Hear That Long Snake Moan," writes that "it was precisely by trying to stop vôdun

I MADE DOZENS
of gourd shakers.
Bead-covered gourd
shaker, also known as a
shekere (right);
rattles, bells,
blocks (below).

that, for the first time in the New World, African music and dancing was presented both for Africans and whites as an end in itself, a form on its own." By separating the music from its religious intent, the century-long gestation began that would ultimately produce the dominant popular musical styles of the twentieth century – jazz, the blues, rhythm and blues, and rock and roll.

The dances in Congo Square came to an end in 1875 with the enactment of the first Jim Crow laws forbidding blacks to assemble freely. These were explosive years for America. It seemed that something much larger than just a war had ended. Almost overnight a whole way of life, the old America of rural farmers, clergymen, and wealthy traders, had disappeared as the industrial revolution took hold. Factories multiplied along the river banks, enormous steel and concrete cities literally climbed into the air.

A new soundscape was born, my soundscape, the auditory chaos of industrial urban noise. And it was out of this soundscape that the backbeat emerged, its first manifestation appearing in those New Orleans brass bands – African rhythms and African sensibility channeled through the unfamiliar instruments of the American marching band – and in the syncopated ragtime of Scott Joplin. The front line of these bands consisted of trumpet, clarinet, and trombone, but sitting in the back, propelling this new beat, was an invention that to my mind rivals those of Henry Ford and Thomas Edison. I speak of course of the drum set.

I like to think that the polyrhythms were so deeply embedded in the African-American consciousness that one of the first things blacks did, after gaining their freedom, was set about remedying their impoverished condition vis-à-vis percussion. There were no drum ensembles in America, not even in New Orleans, nor were there probably any master drummers left. The specifics of the West African rhythmic tradition were lost, except for in the secret societies that still followed vôdun. All that remained was an urge that, once freed, satisfied itself by creating something totally new, a polyrhythmic instrument that one person could play handily.

The instrument's early virtuosos – Baby Dodds, Zutty Singleton, Chick Webb, Gene Krupa, Jo Jones – were all players who explored and extended the voice of the instrument while still fulfilling the rhythmic needs of the music. For instance, up until the forties most players used the bass drum to mark all four beats in a bar, while after the war, spurred by drummers like Kenny Clarke and Max Roach, the beat-keeping role was assumed by the top or ride cymbal, while the bass drum emerged as an accenter, a way to elicit sudden maximum percussive effect – "dropping bombs" was the slang for it.

In West Africa it is said that every drum has its rhythm and every rhythm its dance. In America the novel African-American rhythms quickly inspired new dances. The Charleston, Lindy, Jitterbug, Black Bottom – all emerged from the early experiences of audiences whose bodies were responding to this music for the first time.

I remember exactly what I was doing when the backbeat first affected me, making me want to dance, dance, dance. I was working in a public pool as a junior lifeguard and the older lifeguards had the radio tuned to a station that played "race" music. Little Richard. Chuck Berry. Elvis. Buddy Holly. It was irresistible, this music. It just drew you in. You had no choice.

Looking back on the early years of rock and roll now, I can see why the adults were scared. The screams, the ecstatic states, the hysteria – this music had a power that adults didn't understand. We didn't even understand it ourselves, but we weren't as scared of it as they were. When I think back on the tens of thousands of garage bands that sprang up as rock took hold I realize now it was one of the most powerful explosions of art this country has ever experienced. Suddenly it was cool to get together with a group of guys and not play sports, not do anything competitive, but to get together because you had discovered that by sharing musical energy something incredibly stimulating happened.

The group of guys I joined up with in 1967 came from all over the musical map. Jerry Garcia came from bluegrass. Bobby Weir from folk. Phil Lesh was classical. Pigpen the blues. Billy Kreutzmann was pure rhythm and blues, and I came from military drumming and jazz. I don't think that any of us could have predicted that the trip would last twenty-five years. But I think each of us recognized that there was a peculiar resonance that happened when the six of us got on stage to share sound, that we fit together in a way that truly was greater than the sum of the parts.

The music we have evolved from this blending is our collective sound – Grateful Dead music. And it only happens when all of us play together. It's never as strong when we play the songs individually. It's as though each of us has a piece of the map, of the territory. Sometimes I think of what happens in a shamanistic sense of embarking upon a collective journey in which we are all allies. Other times I think of our music as something almost organic that we've grown over the past twenty-five years, a living entity that exists in another

time-world, in what Blacking would call "virtual time," and that can only be accessed when all of us are on stage.

None of this was planned. It was something we began exploring in the sixties: the use of sound to create a collective experience, mostly for the sheer pleasure one gets from being around resonance, in whatever form.

I think of this as my day job. Eighty times a year I walk out onto the stage, which is a kind of sacred space, I suppose, and I strap myself into an enormous state-of-the-technology machine, a big virtual-time robot, whose sonic payload is mind-boggling. And then I feed this machine rhythm and noise, at the same time carrying on a conversation with five other sound sharers.

The Dead Heads read all sorts of meaning into the form this conversa-tion takes, but up on stage it's almost totally intuitive. The unexpected is still courted; magic won't happen unless you set a place at the table for it. On a really good night there's an extraordinary sense of danger and adrenaline in the music. When you're playing you think you're the only one keeping it together. Then when you stop playing and the thing doesn't immediately fall apart you realize everyone is holding on, everyone's got a piece of it, but still none of them are holding on real tight. The potential of musical embarrassment — disaster — is always there.

And yet so is the other thing. The Magic Ride. The groove.

The other night I woke up at three o'clock and again at five. I had a seven o'clock call for an afternoon show in Los Angeles. Afternoon shows are rare. Usually we play at night in outdoor stadiums, the crowd a surging anony-mous force field beyond the dazzle of the stage lights. But when we play during the day suddenly we see the audience, on this particular hot afternoon forty thousand of them.

Joe Campbell came to one of our shows and remarked to me afterward that we were a myth happening in real time. "This is what the Dionysian rites must have been like," he said. In Africa musicians are never possessed by the spirits they call down with their rhythms, so what possesses our audience I can never know. But I feel its effects. From the stage you can feel it happening — group mind, entrainment, find your own word for it — when they lock up you can feel it; you can feel the energy roaring off them.

It was there the other afternoon in the hot sun with forty thousand people swaying and dancing. We have played for many more, but that's still a lot of bodies, a lot of energy to have focused on you. It has taken us years to learn how to throttle back in such a charged atmosphere, years to learn that if we patiently feed the rhythms, if we manage to vibrate in time, to resonate, then the big wave will come.

Strike a membrane with a stick, the ear fills with noise — unmelodious, inharmonic sound. Strike it a second time, a third.

In the beginning was noise, and noise begat rhythm, and rhythm begat everything else. When the rhythm is right you feel it with all your senses. The head of the drum vibrates as the stick strikes it. The physical feedback is almost instantaneous, rushing along your arms, filling your ears.

Your mind is turned off, your judgment wholly emotional. Your emotions seem to stream down your arms and legs and out the mouth of the drum; you feel light, gravityless, your arms feel like feathers.

You fly like a bird.

TAILFEATHER
*Woman told them that
the Great Spirit had
commanded them to
build a drum.*

*Drumming
at the Edge
of Magic*
232

CHAPTER FOURTEEN

THE MAKING OF THE DRUM

NE DAY, WHILE I was browsing through the books accumulated in my decade-long burn, the one Tom Vennum had handed me so long ago jumped out at me from its place on the shelf.

The Ojibwa Dance Drum: Its History and Construction.

I remembered Vennum saying he had spent several summers with one of the last of the traditional Ojibwa drum makers. The book seemed benign enough as I flipped its pages. Simple brown wrapper, plain type, pen and ink drawing of a drum on the cover. I sat down and began to read.

The book was filled with the sort of reverence for the drum that I had found in the literature of the Counterplayers. Drums were like people for the

233

The Ojibwa Dance Drum

Its History and Construction

Thomas Vennum, Jr.

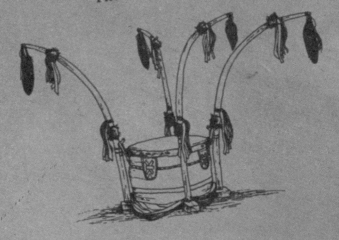

Smithsonian Folklife Studies
Number 2   1982

Ojibwa. They had names and special clothes and were ritually fed. "When tobacco is donated at a ceremony, while the pipe tender receives some of it, the greater share goes to the Drum," Vennum wrote.

All this was familiar from my reading. What was unfamiliar, what I was unprepared for, was the complexity Vennum had been able to discover in what I had thought was such a simple act – the actual physical making of a drum.

Suddenly it struck me – *I'd never built a drum.* I'd been a drummer all my life yet I'd never built a drum. I had repaired them at my father's music store, and I'd built or had built for me dozens of percussion instruments like the Beam and the Beast. But I had never sat down with wood and membrane and made myself a drum. I called up some of my brother drummers and asked them if they had ever built a drum. None had, with the exception of Airto, who told me that once he had killed and skinned a rabbit and made a tambourine.

Vennum's book was as detailed a blueprint as any drummer could want. He wrote that the drum makers of the Ojibwa only built a few drums in their lifetime, usually as the result of dreams that told them exactly what each instrument required. Reading that book was like experiencing a waking dream of my own. Before I had finished it I knew I was going to build myself a drum as soon as possible.

This decision coincided with an invitation from my old friend Hugh Romney, better known as Wavy Gravy. I'd known him since joining the Grateful Dead. He was running a summer camp for children between seven and fourteen, some of them underprivileged kids from the Oakland ghetto, and he wanted to know if I would come and spend three weeks teaching the kids about drums.

Camp Winnarainbow. What do you do at camp? You make things.

I borrowed one of the Grateful Dead's trucks and Ram Rod packed it with instruments from my collection. *Berimbaus.* Bullroarers. Slit gongs. Thirty hoop drums. Enough for every kid in camp who wanted to really experience rhythm and noise.

I had played the teacher in a nonmusical setting only once before, when I taught some retarded children as part of a pilot program on self-esteem. The thought behind the invitation had been that even the most disabled would be able to play concussion sticks and rattles, that virtually anyone could master noise. But I had also wanted to show these kids that they could create rhythm.

I planned to record what happened and then play it back to them at maximum volume — overwhelm them with themselves.

I'd filled different tables with different instruments, rattles on one table, concussion sticks on the other, then demonstrated the sound of each and let the kids choose the one that most appealed to them. At first they were tentative, almost fearful. But the sight of me, acting crazier than any of them, beating on my hoop drum and making animal yells and obviously having a hell of a good time, overcame their resistance. Within five minutes we were a percussion orchestra; within fifteen minutes we'd entrained. Just a brief linking up, but they all felt it, because they all stopped and looked around bewildered. It was amazing to watch. They went from noisy ecstasy back to their old condition in seconds. They no longer trusted the instruments.

The only thing that rescued me was the tape. "Listen to yourselves," I'd told them. "You're a percussion orchestra — you're making music!" And then I cranked up the volume and let them hear themselves. They went mad and started laughing in amazement. One young boy, the catatonic son of an Iranian diplomat, had grabbed a *dumbek* and shut himself in a closet where he drummed and chanted for hours.

Now, at Camp Winnarainbow, I planned to do the same thing. I didn't want to bore these kids with music lessons — it takes years to master an instrument like the *berimbau*. I wanted to give them a taste of something larger, the spirit side. I had jotted down a quote by the Sufi master Inayat Khan that expressed what I was after:

> There are different ways of listening to music. There is a technical
> state when a person who is developing technique and has learnt to
> appreciate better music, feels disturbed by a lower grade of music.
> But there is a spiritual way, which has nothing to do with technique.
> It is simply to tune oneself to the music.

I wanted to take these street kids and tune them to the groove. I wanted to see how fast they'd entrain.

There were close to a hundred kids at Camp Winnarainbow, most in their early teens, both sexes. They lived in huge tipis located around a firepit. The firepit was the camp's meetingplace, where we did exercises every morning and sang songs at night.

NEPALESE
monk with damaru:
*"There is a spiritual
way, which has
nothing to do with
technique. It is
simply to tune oneself
to the music."*
— Inayat Khan

The first thing I did after I arrived at Winnarainbow was walk the whole camp, carrying a *berimbau* with me, looking for the perfect spot. I knew there had to be a perfect spot somewhere among the acres of giant oaks and red-woods or near the lake. There had to be a spot that contained magic, power, a place of such presence that all your senses start tingling, where you feel high, as if suddenly the volume has been turned up, inside you, outside you, everywhere.

No place seized me like that. I ran into Wavy and asked him whether he knew any power spots and he said I might try the hay barn, but it was pretty far. He pointed past the lake, toward the crest of a distant and very steep hill, upon which sat an immense old redwood hay barn. The edge.

It was the most isolated spot in the camp. It felt good to be in this abandoned cathedral-sized building, particularly in the late afternoon when the sun fell at just the right angle revealing all the dust motes and hay chaff dancing in the warm afternoon air.

At the noon gathering I stood up with a hoop drum and announced that I had brought to camp some of our species' earliest musical instruments. Instruments that had been used in very special ways, for very special purposes, and if anyone wanted to learn about these instruments they should meet me there, and I turned and pointed toward the barn.

After lunch I drove the truck up to the barn and carefully unpacked the instruments and placed them around the barn. I wanted to create a garden of percussion. I wondered how many would make the hike. There were a hundred kids in camp; about twenty-five showed up. I demonstrated some simple rhythms and then told the kids to relax, just play, forget being nervous, let the instruments take them where they wanted to go.

It's interesting how long it takes people to entrain. These kids locked up after about twenty minutes. They found the groove, and they all knew it. You could see it in their faces as they began playing louder and harder, the groove drawing them in and hardening. It lasted about an hour. These things have life cycles – they begin, build in intensity, maintain, and then dissipate and dissolve. When it was all over everyone started laughing and clapping. They were celebrating themselves and they were also celebrating the groove. Although they had no words for it, they knew that they had created something that was alive, that had a force of its own, out of nothing but their own shared energy.

When they calmed down I handed them all bullroarers, explaining that this was the first ritual instrument that we had any real information on. The bullroarer is not a quiet instrument. Some bullroarers bark, some howl, others emit terrifying shrieks – the strange, unsettling sound quickly overpowers all your senses. We took the bullroarers outside to play. Their sound was incredible, and the kids quickly got lost in it. But as I observed them, I wondered if anything else was happening. Was the door opening for any of them? Were they feeling it? It occurred to me that I had become a recruiter for the tradition, that the art was using me as a vehicle to reach this next generation of drummers, some of whom were starting to smile.

That's how it begins. Something triggers it and for the rest of your life you are possessed by rhythm and noise. Zakir heard it while he was still in his mother's womb. Airto started dancing to it before he could crawl. I discovered it the first time I hit my father's practice pad with one of his snakewood sticks. It was as if someone had tweaked the pleasure center in my brain. I smiled. I hit the pad again. Although I haven't heard the sound of my father's practice pad in years, I've never forgotten it; at some level of consciousness it is always resonating, it's part of my code.

That sound was the best thing my father ever gave me. I like to think he left it for me unconsciously, that the tradition had also used him as its agent, making him momentarily forget to pack his sticks and pad before deftly slipping out of our lives.

Years after our last dreadful meeting in his office, word had come that my father was dead and that his body would soon be available for viewing at the funeral home. At first I had no interest in seeing Lenny's body or paying last respects. I had removed him from my life, like a bad stain, and it had cost me too much to get clean of him. But even as I was thinking this I was stunned by the realization that I hadn't eliminated Lenny completely from my life. *I still had his snakewood sticks!* This would be my last chance to return them and wipe the slate truly clean.

By the time I arrived at the funeral home, I was so focused on my mission – just put the sticks in the box and split – that I must have appeared crazy to the other mourners, because when Lenny's brother saw me, he gave a startled cry and came rushing toward me with outstretched hands, as though trying to block me out. Behind him Lenny's new family turned to see what the commotion was.

My uncle said something like, "Let's not have a scene, Mickey," and I said, "All I want is ten seconds alone with him. Just clear the room and give me that. I don't want to be here any longer than I have to."

To my surprise, my uncle cleared the room. I walked up to the casket and pulled out the sticks. I meant to just stick them in the coffin and go, but I was suddenly seized by how small and fragile and empty Lenny looked. The drum god. I felt the momentum of my plan draining away. I stood staring at him, trying to hate him.

My hands knew what to do even before my mind caught on to the fact that slowly and elegantly, at the old speed of 110 beats per minute, I was tapping out "The Downfall of Paris" on my father's casket. Drumming him out, honoring that part of him – the best part of him – that was all I could honor. When I finished, I put the sticks in my father's hand and left.

ON THE MORNING OF MY SECOND DAY AT CAMP WINNARAINBOW, I stood up at breakfast and waved one of the fifty copies of Vennum's book I'd brought. I proposed that we build a camp drum, one that would be played for years to come at ritual occasions. Anyone who wanted to participate in this project, I said, should see me this afternoon because that's when we were going to kill the steer.

I had arranged with a local slaughterhouse to do the killing. About a half dozen of us watched as the butcher shot the steer with a 30–30. He'd been patient with us, standing around with an amused smile as we made tobacco offerings to the animal's spirit, assuring it that its meat would feed the poor and its skin would become the voice of a great and powerful drum.

Obtain hide of two-year-old steer.

That's a simple sentence to read, but it doesn't even begin to convey the reality of a sixty-pound hunk of steerhide, dripping with blood, with big gobs of fat still clinging to it. The kids didn't blink an eye, but it nearly made me sick, and it sure depressed me as I contemplated the amount of work it was going to take to reduce this formless bloody mass into a finely stretched and tuned membrane.

I set up operations in a creek bed about a hundred yards from the kitchen. The kitchen was the most popular place in the camp – one thing these kids did a lot of was eat – and I intended to lure as many of these hungry street kids as I could over to my drum pit. The creek we were working in was nearly dry. What made it the ideal spot was a big fallen tree that spanned the creek. We could drape the hide over the trunk and work on it standing up.

So began the long, hot, smelly, endless task of scraping, soaking, stretching, shaving the hairs off, then the fat. By the third day the hide began to stink and the odor attracted bees, who went back and told their hivemates about us. A couple of times we had to grab the skin and run. This added an element of danger that excited the kids even more. I'm afraid we developed a street gang attitude toward the bees. As soon as one appeared he would be assaulted and chased away. Word quickly got back to the hive not to visit our creekbed.

As we worked I told the kids the story of the drum we were making, the Ojibwa pow-wow drum. I told them how, most likely in the 1870s, a vision had come to a Sioux woman named Tailfeather Woman at a moment of profound grief and terror. White soldiers had just massacred her village, killing her four sons and almost killing her. She had managed to escape by hiding in a lake. For four days Tailfeather Woman hid under the lilypads. While she was hiding, the Great Spirit came to her and told her what to do. On the fourth day she emerged from the lake and walked to her village to see who had survived the attack. When the survivors had gathered around her, she told them that the Great Spirit had commanded them to build a drum, saying "That is the only way you are going to stop the soldiers from killing your people."

This was the beginning of the pow-wow, for the Great Spirit had not just given the Sioux a drum, but also a rhythm and dance to go with it – a ceremony. The ceremony spread rapidly among the Indian tribes. Legend has it that Tailfeather Woman herself brought the drum and the dance to Wisconsin, touching off an incident known as the Wisconsin Scare, as the white authorities reacted to "this new Sioux dance which is said to be a religious institution." We were building a power drum, one put on this earth by the Great Spirit.

Every day the crowd in the drum pit grew. Without the limitless energy of the kids I might have given up. I spent mornings in the drum pit, afternoons in the hay barn with the instruments. And very gradually I found myself talking almost as much as I was playing. Up until this point my pursuit of the history of the drum had been largely a private thing; the accumulation of information had been mostly for my own pleasure. This stuff fed me but I'd never really shared any of it with people outside my immediate circle of dance partners. But now I couldn't help myself, it just came flowing out: stories, myths, bullroarers howling in the jungles of Papua New Guinea as the boys underwent the ritual that turns them into men, talking drums calling the *Orisha* down into the bodies of the dancers, Gene Krupa massaging the backbeat.

And as I told these stories and watched the kids absorb them in their tough, suspicious, fourteen-year-old ways, I realized that the Yoruba were right: to keep a spirit alive in this world you need only mention its name. By sharing my feelings about the bullroarer and my stories about it, I was not just feeding these kids, I was also feeding the bullroarer, strengthening its spirit hold on this world.

The Yoruba have the idea of the crossroads, the point where the spirit world and this world intersect. Certain things attract the spirits to a crossroads. One is music, another is stories. The spirits love to listen to both.

At Camp Winnarainbow I saw the answer to something that had been troubling me ever since my visit to the Smithsonian. *Was there any way to save the invisible Counterplayers from the tombs awaiting them in the basements of the museums of the modern world?* Suddenly I could see a way, and it was obvious: by playing the Counterplayer's music and telling their stories. When you do, these fragile powers – the collective spirit of the species – can be nurtured and retained awhile longer. And at that moment I made a commitment to tell the story of the drum to as many people as would listen.

ONE MORNING I LEFT THE DRUM PIT EARLY AND HIKED UP TO THE BARN to sit and think. I wanted something special to consecrate the drum we were making. A ritual of some sort. One that would be both fun and strong enough to link the drum and its spirit side in these kids' minds. I sat in the silence waiting. What came through the door was Joe.

The last time I saw Joe Campbell, a few months before his death, was at the Jung Institute in San Francisco. It was another of our rushed but intense meetings; most of all Joe wanted to pass along all the delicacies he'd saved up since our last meeting and then sample mine. He wanted to entertain. He wanted to toss a few more dried limbs on the fire he happily saw was still burning in my blood. For some reason he began telling me the story of the buffalo maiden, a story he had told thousands of times before. I had heard him tell it superbly, but now he was having trouble remembering the details; he was

THEN WE
stitched the heads together using laces made from the hide. Out of some cloth we made a skirt for the drum — the Ojibwa dress their drums — and decorated it with symbols representing each of the Camp Winnarainbow tipis.

groping for the opening lines. I tried to put him at ease, but he dogged it, wouldn't let it go, and suddenly the rhythm of the myth came back to him, caught him up, and before I knew it Joe had stood and was shuffling through the steps of the buffalo dance, his eyes closed, chanting out the myth as he danced. After he died, it occurred to me that this had been Joe's dance of death. It was as if he had caught a final wind and had ridden it out in glory.

Now I was the one telling the stories. And the story I decided to tell these kids at Camp Winnarainbow was the one Joe had so loved, the story of the shaman's journey, the story of how the shaman rides his drum to the World Tree, summons his allies, and does battle with the dark forces.

It took over a week to reduce the steerhide, using serrated scrapers, to the right thickness. When it was perfect we soaked it in water, then stretched it over a shell and hung it in a nearby tree for four days. As the moisture evaporated from the drumhead, the skin slowly tightened, a process that was intently observed by the kids. Each day the crowd around the drum grew.

I had intended to follow a similar process with the drum body, but it became apparent that we wouldn't have time to chop down and hollow out a tree. It also didn't seem right to take a whole tree for one drum. So we did it the way it had been done by the Ojibwa, according to Vennum.

Obtain one wine barrel. Cut in half.

We placed the wine barrel on the skin and marked how big the two heads should be. Then we stitched the heads together using laces made from the hide. Out of some cloth we made a skirt for the drum – the Ojibwa dress their drums – and decorated it with symbols representing each of the Camp Winnarainbow tipis. The camp had some fine embroiderers who made wonderful trees and animals.

Then we named our drum. All the Ojibwa drums in Vennum's book had the names of their keepers. The Whitefeather Drum. The Pete Sam Drum. The Johnny Matchokamow Drum. Ours was the Winnarainbow Drum.

I began rehearsing the shaman's ritual during the last week. One of the camp counselors became the shaman, and I recruited a number of kids to play percussion. This was one shaman's ritual that was going to be heavy on drums, but otherwise I wanted the kids to imagine that they were somewhere on the North American plains, four hundred years ago. An Indian family has brought a sick relative into the shaman's tipi. The tipi is dark. The family lays the sick person on a cot and retreats. Then the shaman enters and the drumming begins.

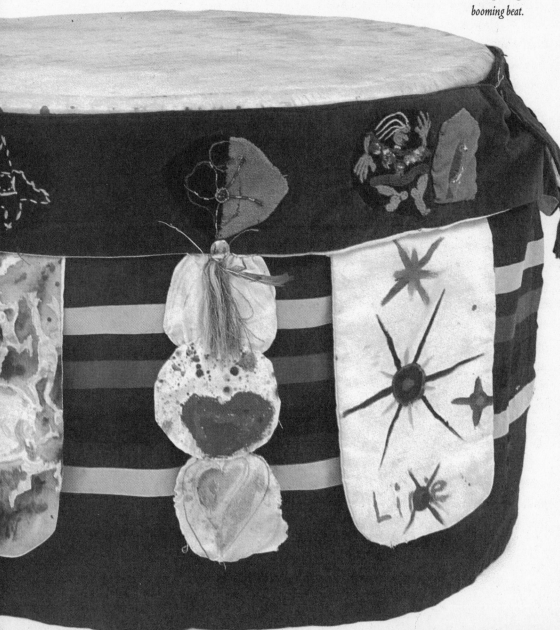

THEN THE
drum spoke, a strong,
throaty, tenor sound,
filling the little
amphitheater with a
slow, pulsing,
booming beat.

The Making
of the Drum

We performed the shaman ritual on the last day of camp, just before the kids went home with their parents. What had started out modestly had grown much grander by opening night. We'd driven at least seventy miles to locate some dry ice, so we'd have a nice smoky fog. We had stiltwalkers in the wings and an actual tree that grew next to the stage – the World Tree. But in the center of it all was the Winnarainbow Drum.

The risk in making a drum is that even though you follow directions exactly, you can still end up with an instrument that sounds like a boot scuffing the pavement. The voice of the drum is a spirit thing, which is why the Ojibwa go to elaborate lengths to infuse their drum with the proper voice.

There was a moment of silence as the lights went down, then the drum spoke, a strong, throaty, tenor sound, filling the little amphitheater with a slow, pulsing, booming beat that was soon joined by an orchestra of rattles and hoop drums.

The counselor who played the shaman was wonderful. He danced on and mimed falling into trance, calling his allies to come and guide him to the World Tree. They came out on stilts. As everyone watched, the shaman climbed the Tree and then went into its roots to battle with the forces of disease.

By this time the percussion orchestra had a wide and thunderous groove going, which I like to think played a part in what followed. One of the counselors had rented from a magic store a theatrical prop that makes a body appear to levitate. When the shaman shouted for the sick person's body to arise healed, the body really *did* rise, and so did the kids in the audience, who all jumped to their feet, their mouths wide open.

For them it was suddenly real. Something had happened that they couldn't explain. It was a trick, of course, but it shattered their expectations and charged their imaginations. Who was going to tell them that a person couldn't rise into the air – hadn't they just seen a steer transformed into a drum?

I still meet some of these kids backstage at shows or on the street. We usually just nod or give each other the high five, rarely stopping to talk. To have built a drum together is probably to be bonded for life; but then to have ridden that drum together – there are no words for that.

E PILOGUE

HALF MILE AWAY across the snow-covered Vermont cornfield, the Federal Express van swung into the driveway of the old farmhouse and a blue-suited driver leapt out.

The last pickup. The last chapters to the coast. A ten-year burn about to come to an end.

"Should we run?"

"Of course."

Flying down the slushy Vermont road, I glanced over at the man running next to me, the prince of words.

Nine months earlier I had shown up in Jay Stevens's life with a load of computer disks that contained my giant electronic Anaconda, that endlessly branching information tree I had begun growing at Karma.

I also brought a powerful computer to replace Stevens's antique one. He stood around bemused as I hooked it up and slid in a disk. Stevens was a bemused sort of guy, very calm, very relaxed, living in a badly insulated farm-house on an out-of-the-way piece of land that his family had owned for centuries. A competent, stable, normal sort of guy, with a wife and kids.

And yet – and yet this guy had written a brilliant book about the history of LSD, a book that was a kind of lucid acid trip in itself. We had been looking for a writer, and my editor had asked me to look through three or four books to see if I liked the rhythm of any of the writing. I read the first paragraph of each, and with *Storming Heaven* I just kept reading. I read the book straight through, then I read it again. Then I got Stevens's phone number and called him up.

"What do you know about drumming?" I asked him.

"Interesting auditory driving technique," he said. I almost dropped the phone.

I soon learned that "auditory driving" was the sort of esoteric delicacy that Stevens savored. He was full of them.

Memes – *there really is a school of thought that's trying to prove ideas are alive, that they're living things using our brains to replicate themselves.*

Flow – *that's because you're in a flow state, right there between boredom and anxiety, mark my words, flow's going to be the place to be in the nineties.*

The first time he met me he told me he'd had his agent insert a special damage clause into his contract in case working so closely for so long with a drummer left him mentally impaired.

You of all people must know what they say about drummers.

And yet I knew. I knew the drum was going to suck him in. I knew it as I slid home that first disk, saw it contained the bullroarer file, and clicked on that.

"Take a look at this," I said. "For a while I really got into bullroarers. I collected all their names, all the myths I could find. I've got hundreds of them here."

Stevens bent down and scanned the list, clicking rapidly through it.

"How many did you say you have?"

"Hundreds."

"And that's just sort of a footnote, right. I mean bullroarers aren't really percussion, are they?"

"You're right. It was just something I got into. One of many. But it's important."

Stevens frowned at the little stack of floppy disks that were piled next to the computer.

"If I printed out one of those, how many pages would I have?"

"Hundreds, maybe thousands."

He began to laugh and moan.

Thus began nine months of intense collaboration, much of the time via the miracle of microelectronics and modems. The Anaconda shed its skin and reproduced, turning into two books, *Drumming at the Edge of Magic* and the more pictorial and encyclopedic *Planet Drum,* which will soon follow. In a sense this book, the one you are now almost finished with, is a long preface to that book.

Whenever the Grateful Dead was in the East I used to spend my free days with Stevens, often arriving in an immense white limo in the wee hours of the morning.

"People are going to think this is a crack house," Stevens's wife, Sara, joked.

She was a sharp one. She noticed what was happening before I did. Late one night we were in the kitchen, drinking coffee, the conversation ricocheting around the way it does at the Stevens house. I was holding forth on something when Sara caught my eye and nodded her head toward Jay. He had a pair of my sticks and he was vigorously beating them on his thighs as he listened to me talk. *Whap . . . whap . . . whap . . . bap . . . bap . . . whap.* He looked up and noticed us watching.

"Hey, what?" he said.

"Omigod," Sara said. "It's like a bad science fiction movie. You two guys are switching brains."

He was the last dancer, I thought, as I watched him running next to me. The last of so many.

The night before, after everyone was asleep, I had sat down at the computer and booted up one of my original disks. I was thinking that maybe this would be the last time, one last climb through the tree, one final trip through the snake.

I rode my drum to the World Tree and all my allies were there.

PEOPLE WHO WERE INVOLVED AND INSPIRATIONAL

Joseph Campbell, who in his retelling of the myths and legends would bring excitement and mystery alive again. *Betsy Cohen,* who introduced me to the electronic information-gathering tool called the computer; she was midwife to the birth of the electronic Anaconda. *Jerry Garcia,* for decades of support and vision shared on the Edge. *Tom Grady,* editor in chief at HarperSanFrancisco, the architect and guiding light of the final version of this book; he found me my last dance partner, Jay Stevens. *Bill Graham,* for blind faith and the seed money for the initial research. *Taro Hart,* for constant joy. *Ruth-Inge Heinze,* who embodies the true spirit of percussion — she served as a guide to Siberian culture and shamanism and was an honest reader of the final manuscript. *Robert Hunter,* who encouraged me and helped to shape the earliest and the last incarnations of this work. *Margie Kidder,* a reader's reader, passionate lover of the written word, and a sharp eye on the edit line. *Stanley Krippner,* an old friend and also a guide throughout all the years of the project's development. *Fredric Lieberman,* my guide to the world of the Ethnos and ally in the gathering of this information; together we stormed the archives of the world's ethnography; he opened many doors and behind those doors were many answers. *Jay Stevens,* the last dance partner, the prince of words; he took the electronic Anaconda and together we spun one hell of a story; he accomplished the impossible. *Thomas Vennum, Jr.,* senior ethnomusicologist, Office of American Folklife Programs, Smithsonian Institution; he was my skeleton key to the rich tradition of the American Indian; when we needed sources or warm bodies worldwide, Tom was there with the right person in the right place, and he was an endless source of support.

PEOPLE AND INSTITUTIONS WHO GAVE FREELY OF THEMSELVES
They understood the spirit at the Edge of Magic.

Remo Belli, designer of the plastic drumhead, which revolutionized the percussion industry, who, with his associate *Lloyd McCausland,* was an enthusiastic early supporter of the book. *John Blacking,* the late ethnomusicologist, who showed me how profoundly music affects community. *Barry Brook,* for his aid and access to the Research Center for Musical Iconography, City University of New York. *Carol and Joe Calato,* of Regal Tip Products, friends who shared information on the process of making drumsticks. *George Carroll,* an authority on little-known but important aspects of military music in the United States. *Nina Cummings* and *Diane Alexander White* at the Field Museum in Chicago. *Sue De Vale,* who gave us information on gong making and gamelan, generously sharing her own lifework. *Alan Dundes,* a king of folklore and our bullroarer scholar. *Hamza el Din,* who taught me about the value of silence, the soft, spirit side of the single-membrane frame drum; together we explored the rhythms of the Nile river and the vast emptiness of the desert. *Leah Farrow,* my mom, who started it all, taught me the rudiments of drumming, and put up with all the noise – she kept the irate neighbors at bay while I pounded, guarding the doors like a lioness, and allowed me to grow as a drummer. *Steven Feld,* ultimate field recordist and musical ecologist, whose work stretched my imagination and allowed me to experience the soundscape of the Papua New Guinea rain forest. *Vic Firth,* a symphonic warrior on the timpani, who provided encouragement along the way. *My Grateful Dead brothers,* for taking me in, putting up with me, and keeping me humble. *The office staff of Grateful Dead Productions,* for their patience and countless hours of faxing, photocopying, coordinating teleconferences, and all. *The Gyuto Monks,* the Tantric Choir, for their peaceful center, their gifts of compassion for all sentient beings, and their awareness of the impermanence of life. *Creek Hart,* who has kept the spirit of percussion alive in our home; he is the groove of the future. *Marty Hartmann,* my uncle, an authority on the drum and bugle corps and World Champion rudimental bass drummer (1939). *Sheryl Heidenreich,* who looked through zillions of archive photographs at Chicago's Field Museum in search of our Holy Grail and then, on her own, wandered the Midwest, in quest of images for the project. *Jeff Hellman,* who kept our computers healthy and happy. *Michael Hinton,* number-one student, now a master of many drumming styles – he embodies the true spirit of percussion on a daily basis and is a constant inspiration. *Naut Humon,* who lives and breathes rhythm and noise. *Zakir Hussain,* who unlocked the secret intricacies governing the pulse — a master drummer who has been a friend, inspiration, and collaborator for over twenty years. *Howard Jacobsen,* a man of imagination who designed the seamless layout of this book. *Mariko Kan,* who graciously opened her house to an invasion of researchers, allowing us to work in the peaceful quiet of the Santa Cruz mountains. *Bryna Kan-Lieberman,* who reminded us where the Edge really is. *Fritz Kuttner,* a grand old man of Chinese idiophones. *Maury Lishon,* of Frank's Drum Shop in Chicago, who supplied the world's drummers for generations. *Alan Lomax,* for his courage, for his role as an activist in stemming "cultural grey-out," and for his incredible spirit and energy in the lifelong pursuit for the preservation of indigenous music and dance. *William F. Ludwig,* who gave us access to his archives on percussion instruments. *Barbara McClintock,* who provided open access with a smile and helping hand at the Jung Institute of San Francisco. *Nion McEvoy,* executive editor of Chronicle Books, San Francisco, who supported the project in an earlier incarnation. *Dennis McNally,* who has provided constant guidance through the media maze. *Barry Melton,* a dear friend who demystified the legal process, kept it simple, and created the framework for this enterprise. *Antonia Minnecola,* a Kathak dancer on the Edge who led me many years ago into exploration of North Indian classical dance. *Ken Moore,* the musical instrument curator who opened doors at the Metropolitan Museum of Art in New York. *Airto Moreira,* my longtime friend and fellow hunter of sounds, who opens the doors of creation every time we play together. *Gordon Mumma,* composer, for lively and informed talks on noise. *Keith Muscutt,* whose sharp eye focused on the details of pre-Columbian art. *Andrew Neher,* an important catalyst, who did seminal scientific work on the question of how percussion and trance are linked. *Babatunde Olatunji,* a much-respected elder statesman of percussion, who was my guide and friend through the complex languages of African polyrhythms and sounds. *Constance Olds,* who culled images for us from the vast collection of the Metropolitan Museum of Art in New York. *Mark Pauline,* for a valuable view of noise. *Charles Perry,* who taught me to play the trap set, giving method to my adolescent madness. *The staff of the Philadelphia Museum. Michael Pluznick,* master craftsman of gourds, who led me into my own contact with santería. *Flora Purim,* in whom a true and sure spirit of music lives — by the incredible sounds of her magnificent voice, she extended my musical horizon to the many voices of nature. *Barbara Racy,* a dance ethnologist who freely shared her visions of the whole world. *Professor Jihad Racy,* consummate musician and ethnomusicologist who led me deep into the Near East. *Andrew Schloss,* who gave his time, knowledge, and support from the beginning; he is the fastest typist I've ever known. *Cameron Sears,* road manager extraordinaire, who calmly bore the logistical burden on the road, allowing me to roam freely through the world's archives, always keeping me on schedule. *Guha Shankar,* who on behalf of this project dove deep into the archives in Washington, pressing beyond the call of duty. *Ram Rod Shurtliff,* a master equipment technician, patient for twenty-five years in rain or shine; he hauled the many drums and books and books and books from city to city, never looking back; a true friend and spiritual advisor. *Huston Smith,* the first person to bring the sound of the Gyüto monks to the Western world, and thus to me. *The Smithsonian Institution,* a deep source of never-ending information about world music and ethnography. *Susan Sommer,* head of New York's General Library of Performing Arts, who steered us to the incredible turn-of-the-century scrapbook of percussion at the New York Public Library. *Sara De Gennaro,* Jay's wife, for all her good advice. *Tovar Vanderbeek,* the technical wizard at CCRMA, and his wife *Lois Vanderbeek,* who guided me through the mainframe there; they were the first to feed the electronic Anaconda. *Hugo Zemp,* who opened up the incredible percussive legacy of the 'Are'Are people from the Solomon Islands for me and, from his work with Africa's Dan people, passed along the "Origin of the Wooden Drum" tale. *Armand Zildjian* and *Lennie DiMuzio,* at the Avedis Zildjian Co., and *Robert Zildjian,* at Sabian Ltd., who generously opened their respective archives.

ARTISTS AND ILLUSTRATORS

David Beck, Kalynn Campbell, David Delamare, Educational Event Coordinators, Carol Lavelle, Leslie Michel, and Nancy Nimoy.

TRIAD PRODUCTION STAFF

Stuart Bradford, Michael Dambrowski, Evana Gerstman, Jon Ianziti, Jerry Pisani, and Karen Sass.

HarperSanFrancisco Production Staff

Kevin Bentley, Wendy Chiu, Terri Goff, Carol Lastrucci, Jim McCasland, Adrian Morgan, Ann Moru, Caroline Pincus, Bernie Scheier, and David Sweet.

Researchers

Their unrelenting enthusiasm and persistence played major roles in the evolution of this work. They may still be out there looking for hortators during the Peloponnesian wars. Come home now; the war is over; it's okay.

Francesca Ferguson, Ph.D., Michael Frishkopf, Jennie Hansen, Kathryn Henniss, Mei-lu Ho, Louise Lacey, Ted Levitt, John O'Connell, David Phillips, David Roche, Nicholas Sammond, and Elizabeth Wright.

360° Productions and "The Edge" Staff
The people who kept it all rolling while I danced.

Howard Cohen, Christine Coulter, Nance Dunev, Mark Forry, Janey Fritsche, Shannon Hamilton, Steve Keyser, Leslie Michel, Merri Parker, John Perdikis, Jeff Sterling, and Karen Tautenhahn.

Project Direction

Dante Anderson, tenacious man of detail, who played an important administrative role in the final stages of this work; *Edith Johnson,* first lieutenant on "The Edge" staff, master of a thousand permissions, tenacious and dedicated office manager, who worked late through countless nights and danced her way through the shark-infested waters of photo research; *Michael Peri,* long-time friend and confidant, who patiently and gallantly brought order to many realms of my life, allowing me to work on the Edge; and *D. A. Sonneborn,* project director, chief of staff at "The Edge," brave warrior, master of a million details and good friend. In the face of insurmountable odds and deadlines, he single-handedly steered the juggernaut upstream under constant fire.

Selected Readings

Blacking, John. *How Musical Is Man?* Seattle: Univ. of Washington Press, 1973. A broad, readable introduction to many important universal questions in world music studies, based on Blacking's extensive field work in South Africa, but including a broad range of traditional, classical, and folk traditions. A cassette tape is available to accompany the musical examples.

Blades, James. *Percussion Instruments and Their History.* Rev. ed. 1970. London: Faber & Faber, 1984. A percussionist's Bible, Blades's lifework is a compilation of data representing several decades of research by an expert classical performer. The sections dealing with non-Western and archaic instruments are based primarily on secondary sources and are useful as starting points for further research. Blades also wrote many of the entries on percussion instruments in the *Grove Dictionary of Music and Musicians.*

Campbell, Joseph. *The Hero with a Thousand Faces.* 2d ed. Princeton, NJ: Princeton Univ. Press, 1968. Originally published in 1949, this extraordinary study may be credited with establishing, almost overnight, the discipline of comparative mythology. Campbell's writing is so attractive and his knowledge so broad-ranging that he managed to reach and maintain a wide audience. Both this volume and *The Way of the Animal Powers* were major inspirations for the current work.

Campbell, Joseph. *The Way of the Animal Powers.* New York: Harper & Row, 1983. Together with the posthumously published *The Way of the Seeded Earth,* this lavish encyclopedia masquerading as a coffee-table book sums up Joseph

Campbell's lifework on world mythology, offering his insights in historical and cultural sequence, lavishly illustrated, and including many texts of myths as well as Campbell's interpretations. An indispensable source.

Chernoff, John Miller. *African Rhythm and African Sensibility: Aesthetics and Social Action in African Musical Idioms*. Chicago: Univ. of Chicago Press, 1979. A searching examination of African music, which has influenced the present book. One of a very few scholarly and well-rounded studies of African musical practice that focuses on the rhythm, music, and dance. A cassette tape of musical examples is available.

de Coppet, Daniel, and Hugo Zemp. *'Are 'Are: un peuple melanésien et sa musique*. Paris: Editions du Seuil, 1978. An extraordinary book about an extraordinary people and their music. Though not yet translated into English, this volume is worth studying both for content and structure. The story of the music and culture of the 'Are 'Are people who live on Malaita in the Solomon Islands, is told in words and pictures by the people themselves, with an appendix by the scholars. Zemp has produced a series of recordings and a full-length film of this music.

Diallo, Yaya, and Mitchell Hall. *The Healing Drum: African Wisdom Teachings*. Rochester, VT: Destiny Books, 1989. An excellent description of the West African rhythm culture from the inside.

Eliade, Mircea. *Shamanism: Archaic Techniques of Ecstasy*. Translated from the French by Willard R. Trask. Princeton, NJ: Princeton Univ. Press, 1972. The classic work on shamanism, predating the recent horde of mystical guidebooks and packed with essential data.

Farmer, Henry George. *Military Music*. London: Parrish, 1950. An authoritative historical survey.

Feld, Steven. *Sound and Sentiment: Birds, Weeping, Poetics, and Song in Kaluli Expression*. 2d ed. Philadelphia: Univ. of Pennsylvania Press, 1990. First published in 1982, this is a prize-winning monograph on the musical culture of a remote Papua New Guinea tribe. An outstanding example of what ethnomusicologists do and a book that has contributed much to the present study.

Gimbutas, Marija. *The Language of the Goddess*. San Francisco: Harper & Row, 1989. A startling and beautiful book by a leading archaeologist, who marshalls all available evidence to demonstrate the predominance of matriarchal religion in Paleolithic Europe.

Halifax, Joan, ed. *Shamanic Voices: A Survey of Visionary Narratives*. New York: E. P. Dutton, 1979. An extraordinary collection of shaman stories from around the world.

Hood, Mantle. *The Ethnomusicologist.* 1971. Reprint. Kent, OH: Kent State Univ. Press, 1982. A personal statement about the values and procedures of doing ethnomusicology, from one of the founders of the discipline in the United States. Engaging and well written, this is a natural follow-up to Blacking's *How Musical Is Man?* for those who want to explore the subject in depth.

Kuttner, Fritz A. *The Archaeology of Ancient Chinese Music.* New York: Paragon, 1990. The major work, summarizing more than forty years of research by this original, brilliant scholar, includes much valuable information on the early history and technology of bells and gongs.

Lomax, Alan. *Folk Song Style and Culture.* Washington, DC: American Association for the Advancement of Science, 1968. A series of papers by the famous folklorist and folk song collector, the man who coined the term "cultural grey-out." His intriguing theory of "cantometrics"—the idea that the shape of a culture is contained in the sounds of its songs—is described here.

McCall, Daniel F. "Mother Earth: The Great Goddess of West Africa." In *Mother Worship: Theme and Variations,* edited by James J. Preston. Chapel Hill, NC: Univ. of North Carolina Press, 1982. In this provocative paper, McCall speculates that in the West African possession trance cultures we can catch an echo of the great Neolithic mother goddess culture that once stretched from Eastern Europe to the Sahara.

Merriam, Alan P. *The Anthropology of Music.* Chicago: Northwestern Univ. Press, 1964. The first thorough exploration of the cultural dimensions of music and music making, Merriam's text is still a classic in the field, read by all aspiring ethnomusicologists. A paperback edition has been published.

Needham, Rodney. "Percussion and Transition." In *A Reader in Comparative Religion: An Anthropological Approach,* edited by William A. Lessa and Evan Z. Vogt, 3d ed. New York: Harper & Row, 1972. Originally a brief contribution to the British anthropological journal *Man,* Needham's essay points out that in a large majority of cases worldwide, percussive music functions to accompany important life-cycle transitions ("rites of passage") and asks why this should be so.

Neher, Andrew. "A Physiological Explanation of Unusual Behavior in Ceremonies Involving Drums." *Human Biology* 34 (1962):151–60. A report on the first laboratory attempts to understand the psychoacoustic mechanisms of auditory driving. Since very little work has been done, before or since, on this problem, the article has been widely misinterpreted and its focused report on a small series of lab experiments has been blown out of proportion by both its supporters and detractors.

Nettl, Bruno. *The Study of Ethnomusicology: Twenty-nine Issues and Concepts.* Urbana, IL: Univ. of Illinois Press, 1983. Fascinating essays that probe most corners of the field, by one of its senior scholars. Recommended as a follow-up to one of the introductory books by Blacking, Hood, or Merriam.

Picken, Laurence E. R. *Folk Musical Instruments of Turkey.* London: Oxford Univ. Press, 1975. The most brilliant monograph on the instruments of any musical culture. Dr. Picken explores in detail every aspect of the instruments, including materials, methods of manufacture, acoustics, performance practice, and repertory.

Price, Percival. *Bells and Man.* London: Oxford Univ. Press, 1983. Like James Blades, Price was a professional musician fascinated by his instruments. His lifework on bells stands as the most important text in the field, and grew out of his extensive articles for *The New Grove.*

Rouget, Gilbert. *Music and Trance: A Theory of the Relations between Music and Possession.* Chicago: Univ. of Chicago Press, 1985. Translated from the French by Brunhilde Biebuyck. The first in-depth study of this subject, Rouget's work builds primarily on his own experiences in Africa, and that of other French scholars in Africa and the Caribbean. Controversial and flawed, it is nonetheless an important book deserving serious study.

Russolo, Luigi. *The Art of Noises.* New York: Pendragon Press, 1986. Translated from Italian by Barclay Brown. Collection of articles by this influential Futurist painter, composer, and instrument inventor, who scandalized with his concerts of noise in the 1910s and 1920s.

Sachs, Curt. *The History of Musical Instruments.* New York: W. W. Norton, 1940. The first extensive treatment of the subject in English; though long out of print and lacking data from recent studies, it remains a major source. Sachs had a truly universal perspective, and he gives extensive coverage to non-Western and pre-modern instruments.

————. *The Wellsprings of Music.* Edited by Jaap Kunst. The Hague: Nijhoff, 1962. Posthumously published, Sachs's last work is also his most stimulating and original. He sums up his lifetime study of world music, and tries to identify major characteristics and styles of human music making. Highly recommended as an introductory text in ethnomusicology, particularly for those with some musical background.

Sadie, Stanley, ed. *The New Grove Dictionary of Music and Musicians.* 20 vols. London: Macmillan, 1980. Along with *The New Grove Dictionary of Musical Instruments* (London: Macmillan, 1984), this is the standard reference work in English, available in any university or large public library. Whatever your musical question, this is the first place to look.

Schafer, R. Murray. *The Tuning of the World*. New York: Knopf, 1977. Shafer, a Canadian composer, explores the world of sound as ecology, environment, and pollution. He creates the concept of "soundscape" to complement that of landscape, and he encourages extensive further work to document contemporary and historical soundscapes.

Taylor, Rogan P. *The Death and Resurrection Show: From Shaman to Superstar*. London: Anthony Blond, 1985. A fascinating exploration of an original thesis that the contemporary counterpart of the traditional shaman is the mass-media entertainer, rock star, actor.

Vennum, Thomas, Jr. *The Ojibwa Dance Drum: Its History and Construction*. Washington, DC: Smithsonian Institution Press, 1982. A detailed cultural study; one of the finest close-ups of a traditional drum, its construction and lore.

Ventura, Michael. *Shadow Dancing in the U.S.A.* Los Angeles: J. P. Tarcher, 1985. Brilliant studies on American culture, including two important pieces on the growth of black music from its African roots.

DISCOGRAPHY

THE WORLD, A SERIES OF RECORDINGS PRODUCED BY MICKEY HART, PRE-sents authentic music from diverse nations and styles, selected for their beauty, power, and significance and recorded in locations ranging from the Nubian Desert to the Arctic Tundra. (For more information about this series, write to: Rykodisc, Pickering Wharf, Bldg. C–3G, Salem, MA 01970.)

The Diga Rhythm Band. *Diga* (RCD 10101/RALP/RACS). Classic percussion from a band of eleven rhythmists, including Mickey Hart and Zakir Hussain, and featuring Jerry Garcia.

Hamza el Din. *Eclipse* (RCD 10103/RACS). Music from the *oud* master from the Sudan.

Dzintars. *Songs of Amber* (RCD 10130/RACS). Folk songs from the Latvian Wo-men's Choir.

The Golden Gate Gypsy Orchestra. *The Traveling Jewish Wedding* (RCD 10105/RACS). A joyous blend of traditional and contemporary music.

The Gyuto Monks. *Freedom Chants from the Roof of the World* (RCD 20113/RACS). The polyphonic chanting of the Tibetan choir, featuring a performance by Mickey Hart, Philip Glass, and Kitaro.

Hariprasad Chaurasia and Zakir Hussain. *Venu* (RCD 20128). Classical flute music from India, featuring *tabla* master Zakir Hussain.

Mickey Hart. *At the Edge* (RCD 10124/RACS). Mickey Hart's companion album to this book, a personal anthology of his lifelong pursuit of the spirit of percussion.

Mickey Hart and Taro Hart. *Music to Be Born By* (RCD 20112/RACS). A soothing, rhythmic soundscape for the birthing environment and beyond, featuring a recording of Taro Hart's heartbeat in the womb.

Mickey Hart, Airto Moreira, and Flora Purim. *Däfos* (RCD 10108/RACS). A musical ethnography of an imaginary country; the adventure of an inner soundscape.

Mickey Hart, producer. *The Music of Upper and Lower Egypt* (RCD 10106/RACS). Recorded during the Grateful Dead's 1978 tour of Egypt.

Ustad Sultan Khan. *Sarangi: The Music of India* (RCD 10104/RACD). The exquisite sounds of the *sarangi*.

Olatunji. *Drums of Passion: The Invocation* (RCD 10102/RACS). A new digital recording by a drum master, featuring eleven percussionists and seven vocalists.

Olatunji. *Drums of Passion: The Beat* (RCD 10107/RACS). A digitally remixed version of *Dance to the Beat of My Drum*.

The Rhythm Devils. *The Apocalypse Now Sessions* (RCD 10109/RACS). Mickey Hart, Bill Kreutzmann, Michael Hinton, and Airto Moreira explore the boundaries of cinematic music.

CREDITS

COVER ILLUSTRATION: Nancy Nimoy. INITIAL CAPS: David Beck. UR DRUM SECTION DIVIDER: Original illustration by Educational Event Coordinators, San Francisco. 4–5: Rosie McGee Ende. 10: Finley Holiday Film, Los Angeles. 13: Herbie Greene. Courtesy of Bruce Howard. 14: Copyright © 1990 by John Werner. 16: The Metropolitan Museum of Art, The Crosby Brown Collection of Musical Instruments, 1889. (89:4.213). Copyright © 1990 by the Metropolitan Museum of Art. 20: Ken Friedman. 24: John Werner. 26: Photo by W. P. Paff. Courtesy of Nan Parnell. 32: Axel Poignant Archive, London. 35: National Anthropological Archives, Smithsonian Institution. 36–37: John Werner. 38–39: Original illustrations by Educational Event Coordinators, San Francisco, after *The New Grove Dictionary of Music and Musicians,* vol. 5, ed. by Stanley Sadie (London: Macmillan Publishers Ltd., 1980). 40: Original illustration by David Delamare. 44: Copyright © 1990 by John Werner. 47: National Museum of Finland. 50: Mickey Hart Archive. 55: John Werner. 58: John Werner. 60: Duncan P. Scheidt. Courtesy of Joachim-Ernst Berendt, from *Jazz: A Photo History* (Frankfurt-am-Main: Wolfgang Krüger Verlag GmbH, 1978). 63 (TOP): Denis J. Williams for *Crescendo International.* 63 (BOTTOM): Schomburg Center for Research in Black Culture, The New York Public Library, Astor, Lenox and Tilden Foundations. 65: Courtesy of William Ludwig. 69: Original illustration by Educational Event Coordinators, San Francisco, after *Four Hundred Centuries of Cave Art,* by Abbé H. Breuil (Montignac, France: Centre d'Études et Documentation Préhistoriques, 1952). 74: Original illustration by Educational Event Coordinators, San Francisco, after a James Bennett drawing, *Thracia,* based on the work of H. Todorova, 1974, and published in Marija Gimbutas's *The*

Language of the Goddess (San Francisco: Harper & Row, 1989). **76**: Louvre, Paris. Copyright © Photo R.M.N. **79**: From *Music: A Pictorial Archive of Woodcuts and Engravings,* selected by Jim Harter (New York: Dover Publications, Inc., 1980). **80**: From *Music: A Pictorial Archive of Woodcuts and Engravings,* selected by Jim Harter (New York: Dover Publications, Inc., 1980). **87**: Mickey Hart Archive. **88**: Mickey Hart Archive. **94**: Ron Bevirt. **103**: Collage by Leslie Michel. Photographs courtesy of Etnomusicologisch Centrum "Jaap Kunst," Amsterdam. **107**: Library of Congress. Photo by Reid Baker. **108**: Shari Robertson. **113**: John Werner. **116**: Courtesy of the Field Museum of Natural History (Neg. #35050), Chicago. **120**: Courtesy of the Field Museum of Natural History (Neg. #32365), Chicago. **125**: Bill Smythe. **126**: Copyright © by Craig Aurness/Westlight. **130**: From *Russolo e l'Arte dei Rumori,* by G. Franco Maffina (Torino: Martano/Vias Battista, 1978). **134**: Jim Marshall. **137**: Jim Marshall. **139**: Jerilyn Brandelius Archive. **142**: Pierluigi Frassineti. **147**: Jerilyn Lee Brandelius. **148**: Margo Moore. **153**: Original illustration by Carol Lavelle. **156**: Todd Cazaux. **159**: Sandy Taylor. **162**: Neg. No. 122773. Courtesy of the Department of Library Services, American Museum of Natural History. **173**: From Uno Holmberg, *Finno-Ugric, Siberian Mythology* (New York: Cooper Square, 1964). **175**: National Museum of Man, Ottawa/Werner Forman Archive, London. **178**: Ken Friedman. **183**: Courtesy of the Field Museum of Natural History (Neg. #A111207), Chicago. **186 (TOP)**: John Werner. **186 (BOTTOM)**: Copyright © 1990 by John Werner. **187**: Copyright © 1990 by John Werner. **188**: Jerilyn Lee Brandelius. **191**: Copyright © 1990 by John Werner. **194**: Photograph by Eliot Elisofon, National Museum of African Art, Eliot Elisofon Archives, Smithsonian Institution. **199**: Vidoc, Department of the Royal Tropical Institute, Amsterdam, The Netherlands. **201**: From *Talking Drums of Africa,* by John F. Carrington (New York: Negro Universities Press, 1969). **205**: Hamburgisches Museum für Völkerkunde. **208**: Courtesy of Biblioteka Narodowa, Warsaw, Poland. **213**: Ken Friedman. Copyright © 1987 by Bill Graham Presents Archives. **217**: Copyright © 1990 by John Werner. **220**: Barbara Racy. **225**: John Werner. *Shekere* by Michael Pluznick. **226**: Frank Driggs Collection. **229**: Bill Smythe. **232**: Original illustration by David Delamare. **234**: John Werner. **237**: Alice Kandell. **243**: John Werner. **245**: John Werner.

ABOUT THE AUTHORS
* * * * *

Mickey Hart has been a percussionist with the Grateful Dead
for almost twenty-five years. In addition, he is the
executive producer of *The World* (Rykodisc), a series of unique
recordings of music from around the world.
His most recent work in this series, *At the Edge,* is a
companion piece to this book. Hart has also composed music for
several television and film projects, including *Apocalypse Now,*
The New Twilight Zone, and *Vietnam:*
A Television History, and he serves on the board of the
Smithsonian Institution's Folkways Records.
Planet Drum, Hart's visual encyclopedia of percussion, will be
published in 1991. Hart lives in Northern California.

Jay Stevens is the author of *Storming Heaven:*
LSD and the American Dream (1987), which *Newsweek* called
"the most compelling account yet of how . . .
'psychedelic' drugs became an explosive force in postwar
American history." His *Lives of the Painters: A Romance of the*
Modern Imagination is forthcoming from HarperCollins.
Stevens lives in Vermont.

Fredric Lieberman, Ph.D., is Professor of Music at the
University of California, Santa Cruz.

A NOTE ON THE TYPE
* * * * *

Drumming at the Edge of Magic was composed at Triad
on the Macintosh. The text typefaces are Monotype Poliphilus
and Blado italic. Display matter is set in versions of the
Monotype Grotesque and Adobe Lithos families.